The Complete Guide to

Ball Python Ownership and Care

Zach Freeman

LP Media Inc. Publishing

Publication Data
Zach Freeman
The Complete Guide to Ball Python Ownership and Care – First edition.
Summary: "Successfully caring for and owning a Ball Python"
Provided by publisher.
ISBN: 978-1-954288-89-8
[1. The Complete Guide to Ball Python Ownership and Care – Non-Fiction] I. Title.

This book has been written with the published intent to provide accurate and authoritative information in regard to the subject matter included. While every reasonable precaution has been taken in preparation of this book the author and publisher expressly disclaim responsibility for any errors, omissions, or adverse effects arising from the use or application of the information contained inside. The techniques and suggestions are to be used at the reader's discretion and are not to be considered a substitute for professional veterinary care. If you suspect a medical problem with your python, consult your veterinarian.

Design by Sorin Rădulescu
First paperback edition, 2023

TABLE OF CONTENTS

Chapter 3

Setting up a Habitat for Your Ball Python 29

Chapter 4

Caring for Your Ball Python 43

Chapter 5

Common Health Issues and Emergencies.....................59

Chapter 6

Breeding Ball Pythons 69

Chapter 7

Troubleshooting and Problem-Solving........................81

Chapter 8

Conclusion and Further Resources...............................89

Writing a care guide about Ball Pythons isn't something I ever thought about doing, but sometimes you stumble upon an opportunity that makes too much sense. My name is Zach Freeman. As a young child, I spent a lot of time exploring outside my rural family home in North Texas. Observing nature made me wildly curious about the wonderful natural world around me. Finding caterpillar cocoons, coming across baby rabbits, and watching geckos skitter along the side of my house every day opened my eyes to the fact that we share our planet with countless beings, each more unique and interesting than the last. My early life inside the house only reinforced this idea.

One of the first pets I can remember having was a Ball Python named Lucky, who was housed in a tank in the bedroom I shared with my older brother. Many nights while I lay in bed, I would watch the dark silhouette of Lucky's body slither along and test the limits of his enclosure. Since then, Ball Pythons and other reptiles have been a treasured component of my life. Years later, my older brother got a pet Ball Python, who he named Barry. Barry would go on to have a positive impact on me growing up. He was calm and happy to curl up and relax on any of our arms. Watching and interacting with him became a major highlight. This experience made me interested in owning my own Ball Python, and fate would see to it that I'd eventually have my wish granted.

Several years later, a man who had been renting a room at my grandma's house moved out with a month or two of rent left unpaid. Before leaving, the man lost a piece of property in the house, or rather, it escaped. A baby lavender albino Ball Python, which he had been housing in a makeshift setup, managed to push aside the grate covering its glass tank and disappear. Enough time had passed that no one expected to see any sign of the snake, least of all the shocked church volunteers who were building a ramp on my grandma's porch. According to what I was told by my mom, they were greeted by the sight of a striking pale yellow snake found in the middle of eating a frog. Whether or not these exact details were true, or they just made for a better story to tell your

Saoirse laying on my lap

teenage son, I'll never know. Sometimes trivial stories and embellishments made in passing end up being the things that really stay stuck in our loved ones' minds.

We ended up keeping the snake after the previous owner used her to pay off his old rent debts. I named her "Saoirse," after the Gaeilge word for "liberty" and the time-honored American tradition of pretending to be Irish. The name ended up being a good fit, as she escaped another two times from the makeshift enclosure I inherited. Unlike Barry, Saoirse was squirrely. Even when being held, she would always try to make her escape from your arms or wherever she was placed. The contrast between Barry and Saoirse showed me that Ball Pythons are unique individuals. Each one has its own personality, independent from any stereotypes we try to assign to the species.

I was lucky to have others around me to rely on for experience and advice about caring for snakes, though there was certainly a lot of trial and error involved as well. In writing this guide, I hope to help Ball Pythons and owners alike by giving them more resources than I had access to. I hope my experiences can help give you advice, calm your fears, and give your Ball Python the best possible experience it can hope for in captivity. For those seeking to better care for their pet Ball Python or those interested in learning more about the topic, I'm happy to do my part in providing a knowledge-first approach to make sure all parties get the most out of this experience.

Introduction to Ball Pythons

Overview of Ball Pythons

Natural habitat and behavior of Ball Pythons

> *Many people call Ball Pythons 'pet rocks' because they are not very active. They are purely instinctual animals, and in the wild, their instinct is to find a burrow and hide in it until they either soil it or shed in it, thus giving away their position as ambush predators. They are stressed by light and movement, so Ball Pythons do best in a small, dark, secure enclosure*
>
> BRIAN CARTER
>
> *BC's Balls*

The Ball Python, whose scientific name is *Python regius*, is a species of nonvenomous snake native to Central and Western Africa. For millions of years, they have carved out a niche as constrictor predators in their savanna, grassland, and open forest biomes. Ball Pythons are mainly terrestrial snakes, preferring to hide in the tall grass directly on top of the earth and underneath it. In the wild, Ball Pythons spend much of their time sheltered in burrows dug by other small animals and in termite mounds. As well as safety from predators, burrows provide

Wild Ball Python sunbathing

consistent temperature, shade, and humidity throughout the day. Oftentimes, unlucky rodent architects will become prey to the same Ball Pythons who go on to occupy their shelters.

During the wet season, when these burrows are flooded and the terrain is soaked, you may occasionally find Ball Pythons temporarily taking refuge in trees. In the more forested regions of the Ball Pythons' range, you can find individuals who spend a lot more time in the trees and have a diet consisting of far more birds than their grassland cousins. This fact about their diets in the wild has created a debate among domestic Ball Python owners over whether birds make a more appropriate food source for their pets. It's important to note over 98% of Ball Pythons that have been exported for the pet trade come from Ghana, Togo, and Benin, which are less forested, sparse, and grassy countries in general.

History of human interaction with Ball Pythons

In their native range, Ball Pythons have had unique and varied relationships with humans since time immemorial. For many people, Ball Pythons are revered as totems or are associated with deities. The Igbo,

for example, revere the Ball Python as a messenger for Eke, the python creator god. Traditionally, the snakes are often treated with great respect and, in many cases, are protected from harm. In some of these cultures and regions, Ball Pythons will be safely relocated back to the wild if they wander into a village or road. If a Ball Python does die or is killed, a funeral may even be held for it, and guilty parties may be punished. Alternatively, there are also plenty of cultures and people in these same areas who have long relied on Ball Pythons for their meat and skin.

Another name in the English-speaking world for this species is Royal Python. The royal moniker harkens back to when rulers would wear these snakes as living jewelry as markers of prestige. The most famous cultural and religious site for Ball Pythons is the python temple in Ouidah, Benin. This has been a site for the worship of Ball Pythons for 800 years and is home to a Ball Python cemetery. To this day, people still come to this temple and pray alongside Ball Pythons for good health and prosperity. Here, you can even go to prison for killing a Ball Python. The most dedi-cated followers of the temple ritualistically carve scars into their faces to resemble Ball Pythons' heat pits. While I don't expect you to go as far as ritual scarification, these examples show just how important Ball Pythons are for some people and emphasize the long and intimate history these reptiles have shared with humans.

Origins of the modern Ball Python pet trade

Ball Pythons first started to gain mass popularity in the exotic pet trade in the 1980s. Their proximity to humans and their docility made them relatively cheap and easy to acquire. After the successful introduction of captive breeding and the explosion of new morphs onto the scene, the Ball Python quickly became one of the most lucrative reptiles in the pet trade. Ball Pythons have many traits that keepers and breeders saw as ideal when encountering and experimenting with the breed. In the recent past, and today, to a lesser extent, people would harvest eggs and gravid (pregnant) females from the wild. In many cases, they would release the females after they laid their eggs. A number of baby Ball Pythons would sometimes also be released after they hatched. While the capture and export of Ball Pythons were for profit, many participating in this market had the foresight to ensure a stable wild population for the future.

Today, a larger part of the market is made up of Ball Pythons bred in captivity, both in their native range and around the rest of the world. Ball Python ranches on the West African coast are now a more likely point of origin for pets than the wilds of that same region. While captive breeding programs have increased competition, an explosion in demand has allowed the export of wild-caught Ball Pythons to remain profitable.

Ball Pythons are sometimes called "royal pythons," but how did they get this illustrious title? Legend has it that Queen Cleopatra VII, the iconic and influential Egyptian queen, wore a Ball Python as jewelry. While evidence of this claim is dubious, the name "royal python" is still widely used to describe Ball Pythons today.

The global demand for Ball Pythons falls short by about 150,000 individuals every year by some estimates. Many Ball Python owners and breeders are opposed to the sale of wild-caught Ball Pythons. Many worry that their endemic populations could be depleted by this practice.

For example, Tom Harbin of Tom Harbin Reptiles advises those interested in purchasing a Ball Python, *"Under no circumstances should you purchase a wild-caught Ball Python."*

While these concerns are warranted, there are many who also argue that the Ball Python pet market creates incentives for people living alongside Ball Pythons to ensure that they're kept alive in the wild. If locals cannot make money exporting live Ball Pythons, then they will likely make money on the skin and bushmeat markets instead. The last thing we want as enjoyers and advocates of Ball Pythons is to see them gone forever. While it may be difficult to control what happens to Ball Pythons in their native range, we can guarantee one thing. As long as there are Ball Python owners and breeders, the species has at least some sanctuary from whatever befalls wild populations.

Anatomy of Ball Pythons

Physical and behavioral characteristics of Ball Pythons

There is a great deal of variety in the Ball Python species. Most Ball Pythons have a base color of brown or tan with black markings. Other colors, like yellow and white, are also common in the domestic pet trade. These markings can be arranged in a variety of ways, including bands, stripes, or blotches. Some Ball Pythons also have a pattern of small, circular markings on their skin, which are called "speckling." In addition to their base color and markings, Ball Pythons can also have variations in color intensity, ranging from very light to very dark. Some Ball Pythons also have a shimmering, iridescent quality to their scales. Overall, the patterns and colors of Ball Pythons are highly variable and can be quite striking.

The name Ball Python refers to the fact that the snake may somewhat curl into a ball when threatened or sleeping. In the wild in Benin, they have been observed to be crepuscular, meaning they are active for a few hours in the evening and a few hours in the early morning. In captivity, it is not uncommon for them to be generally nocturnal. So, as a prospective owner, don't necessarily expect your Ball Python to be out and about on your schedule.

Ball Pythons tend to be relatively docile compared to other pet snakes. Even in the wild, Ball Pythons are unlikely to strike at humans unless threatened. The snakes are largely solitary. Though they can be found nesting together on some occasions, socialization is not something they seek out, and prolonged exposure to other Ball Pythons may lead to higher stress.

"Balling" is a typical behavior exhibited by Ball Pythons and also the source of their name! Coiling up into a ball ("balling") is normal behavior and typically a sign of stress or fear. Ball Pythons use this behavior as a defense mechanism rather than biting or attacking the source of their anxiety. If your Ball Python is frequently balling, check for stressors such as inadequate temperature, inappropriate humidity, or other triggers in its enclosure. At the risk of triggering a rare aggressive display, Ball Pythons should never be forced out of their balled-up state.

Life span and size of Ball Pythons

Ball Pythons can grow to a maximum length of a little over six feet and a maximum weight of about seven pounds. Most Ball Python owners should not expect to see sizes anywhere near the maximum, though. The average male Ball Python is likely to grow up to about three and a half feet, while a female may grow closer to four and a half feet. Most Ball Pythons will be between three and four pounds. One lineage of Ball Pythons, named after the Volta region in Ghana, has been known to exceed five and even six feet in length. Apart from their exceptionally large size, they resemble most other Ball Pythons native to the region.

In the wild, Ball Pythons can be expected to live for about 15 years. Ball Pythons can be expected to live about 25 to 30 years in captivity, though the oldest known Ball Python lived to be 48. As such long-lived animals, Ball Pythons can be lifelong companions and are a serious long-term investment.

CHAPTER 2

Choosing a Ball Python

Finding a Healthy Ball Python

Finding a reputable breeder or pet store

There are a wide variety of resources available for those looking to buy a Ball Python. As large as the Ball Python trade is, you may feel overwhelmed by the number of breeders and sources available. Figuring out where and how you acquire your Ball Python is one of the biggest steps you'll take on the road to becoming a Ball Python owner. As such, it's vital that you do your due diligence to ensure you end up with results that you feel happy and comfortable with. By choosing to get your first python from a breeder, as opposed to acquiring a wild-caught snake, you can better ensure you have greater knowledge of the snake's history, origin, and condition.

Wild-caught Ball Pythons can be far more likely to harbor parasites and may develop an illness due to poor conditions in transit. In fact, many Ball Pythons die in transit due to stress, inadequate

Unlike other species, male Ball Pythons are actually smaller than their female counterparts. Female Ball Pythons generally grow faster and are longer than male Ball Pythons in maturity. On average, female Ball Pythons can reach three to five feet, while males grow two to three feet long.

temperature control, and a variety of other factors. This is one thing to be aware of if you're tempted to import a Ball Python directly from the source. Ball Pythons, being the most widely kept snake, can usually be found locally through reputable breeders.

When searching for breeders, there are several key factors that can give you a clue into whether your chosen source is worthwhile. First, you want to be aware of how long your breeder has been in operation. Brand-new sellers can present greater uncertainty and a higher risk than those who have been long-established and tested through time. To avoid any possible fraud or misfortune, it's best to do your research on how long any breeder or seller has been operating and if they're affiliated with a business. A large number of positive reviews and testimonials, preferably spanning back years, are a great way of verifying a breeder's legitimacy. For larger businesses and established breeders, you shouldn't have to search as long for their credentials as they typically want to present them front and center if they reflect well on their business.

Some companies and websites do not breed the snakes they sell; instead, they buy from breeders in bulk, then resell the snakes to potential owners. Buying from a large bulk business can be much more convenient for a first-time owner. Such businesses often act as one-stop shops for

all your Ball Python setup needs, offering starter kits, terrariums, and a wealth of information on how to care for your python. You can also find a much greater variety of Ball Python morphs in these larger market-places. Payment plans and overnight guaranteed live shipping are also possible benefits that many of these companies offer. Because they act as middlemen between breeders and buyers, they are less likely to give you comprehensive information about the lineage and particular history of the Ball Python you're buying.

Another major factor to consider is that, despite any guarantees, there are countless horror stories of owners who received dead or near-dead reptiles from these large retailers. When shipping an animal any large distance, there is always a chance that something could go wrong. Many customers who buy from these sites do receive perfectly happy and healthy pets with no issues, but the worst-case scenario is something to keep in mind when considering buying from these kinds of sellers. While more convenient, shipping a reptile often entails a greater degree of uncertainty and chance. If you're interested in larger, mostly online retailers and are willing to accept the added risk, some places to start looking are XYZ Reptiles, CB Reptiles, Wilbanks's Captive Reptiles, and similar traders. Of course, always do your research before making your selection to determine what seller and python are right for you.

If you value having more information about your Ball

Did you know that no two Ball Pythons look exactly the same? Like a human's unique fingerprint, each snake displays an original pattern on its scales. While some Ball Pythons may appear similar to others, some have bold or unusual genetically inherited patterns called "morphs." Common morphs include Albino, Spider, Pastel, Ghost, Clown, and Champagne. The rarest morph is the Stranger Ball Python, first bred in 2012.

Python's background, then you may prefer to buy directly from a breeder. Many conscientious owners also prefer to verify that their pets were bred and brought up according to high-quality standards to ensure that they receive the healthiest possible snake. A guarantee of this knowledge is not typically possible with large online retailers, though you may infer the quality of breeders and their facilities by the typical review left on their site. Maintaining a relationship with a trusted local breeder may also guarantee that you have a more thorough and interpersonal source of advice at your disposal.

Buying directly from a breeder can also be cheaper than sourcing your Ball Python through a larger business, especially if you manage to find what you're looking for locally. Websites like Morph Market can help you connect directly to breeders online and find stores near you. Online forums like ball-pythons.net and reptileforums.co.uk, alongside Ball Python hobbyist Facebook groups, can also be useful tools in tracking down a trustworthy breeder near you. Garrick DeMayer of Royal Constrictor Designs had this to say about buying directly from breeders. *"Finding the right Ball Python is mostly about finding a reputable source of high-quality captive-bred-and-born Ball Pythons. Generally, it is best to purchase directly from a breeder. A good breeder will be able to provide the hatch date/age and what the snake is feeding on. It is a good idea to do a little research on the breeder before buying the snake. It is easy to find reviews online, and it can save lots of headaches from buying from the wrong source."*

Major brick-and-mortar retailers like PetSmart and Petco also sell Ball Pythons, but many owners and breeders steer clear of these establishments. In many owners' eyes, they have a reputation for sourcing their snakes from unreliable breeders and a tendency to keep Ball Pythons in conditions where they do not receive the best of care. When buying from a location like this, there may be a greater risk that you might purchase a

*Photo Courtesy of
Elite Exotic's BP*

sick or unhealthy snake. Some owners consider buying from these stores as a sort of rescue.

Choosing a visually healthy snake

> *As a first-time owner, one should always look for clear eyes, smooth scales, and a generally healthy body weight when selecting a Ball Python. Snakes that aren't in optimal health can produce an entirely different set of issues for a new keeper to deal with than a healthy and thriving animal.*
>
> PAMELA TRENTHAM
> *Python Passion*

If you're looking to purchase a problem-free animal, having the chance to view a Ball Python in person before you buy it is ideal. A healthy Ball Python will be plump with a barely visible spine and a rounded body. The spine should appear straight and even, without any twists or significant bulges. If a snake is not in the process of shedding or about to shed, its eyes should be bright and clear, and its scale should be shiny and popping with color. A dull or cloudy appearance is natural when a snake is shedding but can also be a sign of poor health. Red or dark unnatural discoloration is usually a bad sign.

Ensure that the snake does not have liquid or mucus built up or dripping from its mouth or nostrils. A wheezing sound while breathing, labored breathing, or any noticeable unusual sounds can suggest respiratory issues. A Ball Python should also be active when being handled or at periods throughout the night. When alone, they will often be in their burrow or beneath their hide rock. A snake may be lethargic, hyperactive, or act strangely due to illness or elevated levels of stress. Be wary of any unusual or wobbly movements when first viewing a Ball Python.

Albino Morph

Bamboo Morph

Bananna Morph

Bumblebee Morph

Enchi Morph

Cinnamon Morph

Fire Morph

Ball Python Morphs

What are Ball Python morphs?

Morph is a word used to refer to the appearance and heritage of certain Ball Python phenotypes outside of the normal brown and black coloration and pattern. From the beginning of the Ball Python pet trade, pythons with unique features or atypical colors and patterns have been highly valued. Many morphs can be found naturally in the wild as a result of genetic mutation. The area surrounding Abomey, Benin, is where a good deal of the naturally occurring morphs or their genetic stock seem to be from. Future breeders quickly saw the appeal of these aberrant Ball Pythons, and morphs became a very big part of the industry. Under captive breeding, countless new colors, patterns, and traits have been discovered and bred into unique lineages. New morphs are still being developed every day.

Breeders and owners have developed their own vocabulary and, when speaking about their trade, often use language that may take you back to your high school biology class. "Super" refers to a Ball Python with two copies of any particular morph allele, meaning it's homozygous. If you breed two of the same morphs together, then statistically, about 25% of their offspring will end up being super. Supers can look completely different from heterozygous or het Ball Pythons. As an example of how confusing Ball Python genetics can be, if you breed any two morphs in the blue-eyed leucistic complex, or BEL, you can end up with a stark-white, blue-eyed snake. Any of the following morphs have the potential to create blue-eyed leucistic Ball Pythons when bred together.

- Bamboo
- Butter/Lesser
- Mojave
- Russo Het Leucistic
- Phantom
- Mystic
- Mocha
- Special
- Daddy Gene

Mojave Morph

Pastel Morph

Phantom Morph

Pinstripe Morph

Piebald Morph

Spider Morph

Sunset Morph

List of different morphs

Listed below are some other examples of common morphs you might encounter when doing research for your first Ball Python.

- Spider
- Banana
- Albino
- Piebald
- Pastel
- Axanthic
- Mojave
- White
- Scaleless
- Sunset
- Bumblebee
- Clown
- Fire
- Pinstripe
- Enchi
- Purple Passion
- Black Pastel
- Cinnamon
- Lavender Albino
- Lesser
- Black-backed
- Butter
- Pewter
- Vanilla
- Mystic
- Stormtrooper
- Ivory
- Ghost
- Coral Glow
- Champagne
- Red
- Lemon Blast
- Highway
- Dreamsicle
- Yellow Belly
- Woma
- Phantom
- Candino
- Chocolate
- Spotnose
- Candy
- Tiger
- Super Blast
- Acid
- Ringer
- Blue-Eyed Leucistic
- Fire Ivory
- Blue-Eyed Lucy
- Bongo Pastel
- Ghi

This massive blur of bullet points and names is only the tip of the iceberg. Currently, over 7,500 morphs have been documented, and more are being made all the time.

Price ranges for different morphs

While Ball Python morphs may be stunning in appearance and offer variety from typical coloration, potential owners should be aware of extra considerations that could be at play. Morphs have varying levels of rarity, and as a result, many morphs may be more expensive than snakes with a typical phenotype. One of the least expensive morphs is the pastel, which can sell for under $100 in many instances, with some breeders selling these snakes for as little as $40.

Ball Python breeding is still an emerging science, with the capacity for new morphs always present. New and extremely rare morphs can have a price tag peaking in the tens of thousands of dollars. One lavender albino Ball Python sold for $40,000 when the morph was created, making it one of the most expensive snakes ever sold. Today, lavender albino morphs can sell for as little as $250. Blue-eyed leucistics, which were mentioned earlier, range from about $800 to $1,000.

Potential health issues of certain morphs

Some morphs present a challenge even for experienced owners due to their unique genetic maladies. The small gene pool present in some morph populations has made the occurrence of certain genetic disorders much more common than in others. Famously, spider Ball Pythons are often afflicted with a central nervous system disorder that causes trembling, dubbed the "spider wobble" by breeders. In its most severe cases, the spider wobble can cause severe distress in the snake and significantly inhibit its coordination and ability to move and eat safely. While its coloration and web-like dark markings make it an attractive morph, it has a high potential to suffer a worse quality of life and require greater specialized care than other morphs.

Other morphs, like bumblebee, woma, and champagne, can also suffer from this disorder. Any morph crossed with or deriving from a spider base is likely to have some degree of wobble. Crossing a spider morph with a sable morph tends to make the severity of wobble even worse. The super spotnose morph is also known to have a severe wobble. The International Herpetological Society has banned the sale of Ball Pythons with the spider gene at any of their affiliated events, yet the morph can still be bought and sold by non-affiliated breeders.

Kinking is another health issue associated with another morph, caramel Ball Pythons. Kinking is similar to scoliosis in humans and manifests as hard bumps or curves in the spine. It can impact digestion and movement, even fatally if severe enough. Caramels are known to have several other health issues as well. Additionally, fertility issues in some morphs, like female deserts, may present a challenge if you intend to breed your Ball Python. Albino Ball Pythons, which are one of the most common morphs you'll encounter, have increased sensitivity to sunlight and can often suffer from poor eyesight. Their poor eyesight can make albinos more nervous and fearful when being handled, which should be taken into consideration when selecting a Ball Python.

All in all, these are only a few examples of the potential genetic disorders and complications that are common in certain morph lineages. It's vital that you, as a prospective Ball Python owner, are knowledgeable of any potential heritable issues that may be present in any morph you consider purchasing. Otherwise, you could end up with a snake that you are not prepared or equipped to care for.

Accompanying or additional aesthetic differences in some morphs

Other traits, like eye size, eye color, and mouth shape, have also been selected for breeding. Some breeders have selected for tiny eyes in Ball Pythons, while others have selected for large "bug eyes." Specific eye colors are also a desired trait for some breeders. Some morphs, like the leucistics mentioned earlier, are known for having blue eyes, for example. An upward curvature of the snout has also been bred into some morphs, sometimes unintentionally and sometimes not. This curvature is often referred to as a duckbill and can be common in some morphs like the super black pastel and super cinnamon. It can also occur accidentally as a result of problems during incubation. These traits are similarly controversial among owners and breeders. Some argue that deformities like these negatively affect the snake's day-to-day life and functions, though others disagree and prefer these snakes aesthetically. Whichever is the case, be prepared for the chance that any physical difference with your Ball may uniquely contribute to its care and health.

Should You Get a Ball Python?

Are Ball Pythons the right pet for you?

All the information presented so far has probably got you thinking a lot already. Selecting and caring for Ball Pythons, or any reptiles, might be more complicated than some people initially think. With their long life spans, Ball Pythons are also a long-term commitment—one that you may even have to pass on to your children. You must be prepared to give your Ball Python the care and attention it needs for the next 40 years of your life.

Knowing what to expect with Ball Pythons

> *There is a saying that a hiding Ball is a happy Ball. Ball Pythons are very easy to keep, as they only have three basic needs: proper heat, proper humidity, and most important of all, proper security. For the first 24 hours in your care, it's normal for the snake to be out exploring and crawling around. But if it is still doing this days later, this can be an indication of stress—usually involving the use of lights or size of the enclosure.*
>
> BRIAN CARTER
>
> *BC's Balls*

When taking that first step, you should think about your own lifestyle and whether you have the time and resources to properly care for a Ball Python. These reptiles require regular feeding, enclosure cleaning, and handling to maintain their health and well-being. You should also consider whether you have the space to set up a suitable enclosure for your Ball Python, as they need a secure, appropriately sized, and temperature-controlled space to live. Finally, you should consider the financial commitment of owning a Ball Python. These reptiles have specific dietary and environmental needs that can be expensive to meet over their life, and you will also need to be prepared to budget for regular veterinary care. Some pet owners find that this tradeoff is not worthwhile for them. Ball Pythons spend most of their time sleeping, away from view. They are fairly low-energy pets, which some owners do not find exciting or glamorous enough.

When asked, *"Do Ball Pythons make a good pet for a first-time snake owner?"* Brian Carter of BC's Balls gives an excellent reply. *"It really depends on what first-time owners are looking for in their first snake. Many call Ball*

Pythons 'pet rocks' because they are not very active. This is a double-edged sword because if owners want a pet they can see all the time, a display animal, so to speak, then a Ball Python might not be right for them. Ball Pythons do best in a dark, small, secure enclosure and are stressed by light, movement around them, etc. They are purely instinctual animals, and in the wild, their instinct is to find a burrow and hide in it until they either soil it or shed in it, giving away their position of being an ambush predator."

Ball Pythons are among the most popular pet snakes due to their gentle dispositions and lack of venom. These snakes skyrocketed in popularity during the 1990s and remain beloved pets today. Though some consider Ball Pythons to be excellent beginner snakes, proper education about Ball Python ownership can go a long way toward preventing illness and injury for you and your snake.

You should also consider your own personal experience and comfort level with reptiles. Ball Pythons are generally docile and easy to handle, but if you have never owned a reptile before, it may take some time to get used to their unique needs and behaviors.

What might go wrong if you aren't prepared for your Ball Python

No one likes to think about worst-case scenarios, but there are several negative outcomes that might occur if you get a pet Ball Python that you are not prepared for. First and foremost, Ball Pythons require a specific habitat and diet to thrive. If you do not provide these necessary conditions, your Ball Python could become sick or even die. Not only is this cruel and unfair to the snake, but it is also likely to take a toll on you as an owner, emotionally and financially. If you are not proactive in preventing problems, vet bills can be quite expensive, and if you are not prepared for these costs, you may struggle to provide for your pet. It is important to do thorough research and be prepared for the commitment of owning a Ball Python before bringing one into your home.

Ball Pythons need frequent monitoring and attention to ensure their safety. Malfunctioning heating pads can cause burns, which can worsen over time. Improper ventilation, poor temperature control, and a lack of a proper cleaning schedule can end up making your pet sick. Checking up on your snake regularly can help you do damage control and allow you to correct any problems that might arise due to any lapses in judgment or experience.

The worst thing that pet owners can do if they find they no longer want or are no longer able to care for their pet is to release it into the wild. If released into an ecosystem where they are not native, Ball Pythons could potentially compete with native species for resources. In addition, releasing a pet into the wild is often considered to be inhumane, as the animal may not be able to survive on its own in an unfamiliar environment. Instead, it is important to properly care for a Ball Python as a pet, and if the owner is no longer able to care for the animal, to find a responsible home or surrender the animal to a reputable reptile rescue or sanctuary. The only surefire way to prevent this problem, of course, is to not get a pet you are not prepared for or will get bored of.

Ultimately, the decision to get a Ball Python (or any pet) should be based on careful consideration of your resources, lifestyle, and ability to

provide for the animal's needs. If you are an experienced reptile owner and have the time, space, and resources to care for a Ball Python properly, they can make wonderful pets. However, if you are unsure if you are ready for the commitment or do not have the necessary resources, it may be best to choose a different pet.

We've seen what can happen with released or escaped pets with one of the Ball Python's larger cousins. Since the 1990s, the Burmese Python has become a harmful invasive species in the Florida Everglades. These non-native snakes have established a population in the region and are having a significant negative impact on native wildlife. Burmese Pythons are known to prey on a wide variety of animals, including mammals, birds, and reptiles. This has led to significant declines in the populations of many native species. Many small- to medium-sized mammals cohabiting with Burmese Pythons have seen their populations decrease by over 90%. In addition to the ecological impacts, Burmese Pythons are also a safety concern for humans.

While Ball Pythons may not be as outwardly menacing, the consequences of irresponsible animal stewardship can be cascading and far greater than we might expect. Responsible pet-keeping and heavily weighing your options when deciding what pet is right for you is the best way to benefit yourself, your pets, and your environment in the long run.

Why Ball Pythons are still great pets

> *Ball Pythons are awesome snakes to work with. They are generally very calm and handleable. They stay small compared to most species of pythons and can easily be kept in a moderate-sized enclosure for their entire life. They also come in a huge assortment of colors and patterns, which makes them visually interesting.*
>
> **GARRICK DEMEYER**
> *Royal Constrictor Designs*

Overall, owning a Ball Python can be a rewarding and enjoyable experience, but it is important to carefully consider all these factors before making the decision to bring one into your home. Once you have confirmed that you are prepared and committed to caring for a Ball Python, you can really take your first true step into your future with these amazing animals. Don't let all my prior warnings scare you too much. While Ball Pythons are a major commitment, they are a worthwhile one for owners suited to them. Ball Pythons can be very personable and gentle animals. Owners who are handling a snake for the first time will find that few other snake species provide the same level of safety and accessibility for handling and interacting with their pet as Ball Pythons do. Discovering more about their unique personalities and individual attitudes will become a daily joy for those willing to put in the time. Additionally, owners of Ball Pythons will find themselves constantly captivated by the beauty and diversity of colors and patterns that these snakes exhibit, making every day a new discovery.

CHAPTER 3

Setting up a Habitat for Your Ball Python

Setting Up a Habitat for Your Ball Python

Choosing the right size and type of enclosure

> *The biggest mistake I see with Ball Pythons is their enclosure size. I think the biggest misconception about them is that they need a lot of space, when in reality, this only makes it harder for them to acclimate and feed consistently. For either sex, a juvenile Ball Python can be housed in a 10-gallon tank for over a year. Once they've reached 700 to 800 grams, males can be moved to a 20-gallon tank for life, while females can be moved to a 20-gallon tank when they reach 1800 to 2000 grams, at which point a 40-gallon tank would be more appropriate.*
>
> BRIAN CARTER
>
> *BC's Balls*

When choosing an enclosure for your Ball Python, it is important to consider the size and needs of your snake. A properly sized enclosure provides your snake with enough room to move around, explore, and thermoregulate (regulate its body temperature), as well as enough space to maintain its humidity needs. A 10-to-20-gallon

enclosure should be suitable for hatchlings and juveniles. Adult Ball Pythons typically reach a length of three to five feet, so a minimum enclosure size of 40 gallons is recommended. Many owners prefer to keep their Ball Pythons in much larger enclosures, up to 120 gallons or four feet by two feet by two feet.

Keep in mind that Ball Pythons require much more horizontal space to stretch out than vertical space. A commonly cited rule is to make sure

the side length of your enclosure is at least the same length as your snake so that it can fully spread out. Decades of Ball Python husbandry have shown that a variety of different setups can contribute positively to your pet's care and quality of life. Part of owning a Ball Python is being reactive and aware of what setup is best for your needs as well as your pet's.

A larger enclosure will provide more room for your snake to move around. However, it's important to consider the snake's sense of security when choosing a living space. In the wild, Ball Pythons are often eaten by larger predators like cobras, birds of prey, and carnivorous mammals. Wide open spaces may make them feel more vulnerable. To counteract this, it's important to provide plenty of hiding spots and cover for the snake. Larger enclosures will generally also lose heat and humidity more quickly.

Not only will you have different sizes to choose from when deciding on your Ball Python's housing setup, but there are also a variety of different materials and styles. Plastic, glass, and PVC are three of the most commonly used types of enclosures used for Ball Pythons.

Plastic tubs have several advantages. They are lightweight and easy to move around, which can be especially useful for cleaning or any reorganizing you have to do. Plastic is also a good insulator, helping to maintain stable temperatures and humidity in the enclosure. Plastic tubs are often the least expensive option for housing your Ball Python. If you choose to use a plastic tub, ensure that it has an adequate number of air holes and a latching lid. Plastic is also more vulnerable to the elements. Extremely high temperatures can melt or warp plastic.

Glass terrariums provide clearer visibility. However, they are heavier and are often more expensive than plastic tubs. Secondhand glass tanks, likely used as fish tanks or other reptile enclosures, can be found for low prices, though they need to be cleaned thoroughly and inspected for any cracks or damage before becoming your Ball Python's long-term home. Glass tanks will offer you the best visibility of your pet, though, as mentioned earlier, this may be a negative point from the snake's perspective. Most glass tanks come with a detachable mesh screen for a lid. Like plastic tubs, you must ensure this lid is properly secured and latched, as most Ball Pythons will be able to push off an unsecured mesh screen with ease.

Glass will become smudged more easily and can start to look dirtier faster than many of the other options, so you may need to devote a little more time to spot-cleaning. Glass tanks are the worst option as far as heat and humidity retention. If you chose a glass tank, be prepared to spend much more time maintaining the proper conditions for your Ball Python.

PVC (polyvinyl chloride) enclosures are another option that's quickly become popular among Ball Python owners. They offer many of the heat- and humidity-retaining qualities of plastic while being much more aesthetically pleasing. PVC enclosures are often closed on three sides with a clear front for viewing. A typical PVC cage will have a sliding or hinged front-facing door, often with small holes or ports for ventilation. Be prepared to spend a pretty penny on PVC enclosures, though, as they are one of the most expensive options. You can find many PVC enclosures built specifically to cater to the needs of Ball Pythons and similar reptiles.

Several other materials, such as sealed wood or melamine, can also be suitable options with the right attention and research. Owners may even choose to build the enclosure themselves or pay to have an enclosure custom-built.

Providing the appropriate substrate and furnishings

Hide boxes are a must with this species. They're known for being finicky eaters, which is generally a result of stress, and tight, secure hide boxes with only a single opening provide them the most security. I recommend steering clear of those half-log hides, as I've found that most Ball Pythons hate them and will not use them.

PAMELA TRENTHAM

Python Passion

Choosing the correct substrate is another key factor in making a space that's safe, comfortable, and convenient for your Ball Python. There are many kinds of bedding to choose from when setting up your enclosure. Each option has its own list of pros and cons, with owners and breeders finding success with a variety of available substrates.

Listed below are some of the most common types of substrates preferred by Ball Python owners.

- Aspen bedding
- Coconut soil/husk
- Cypress mulch
- Newspapers
- Paper towels
- Paper cage liners
- Bioactive substrates
- Orchid bark
- Shredded paper

Each type of substrate has different advantages and disadvantages, working best for different setups and desired outcomes. Most of them can be easily found at your local feed store or online.

Substrate made from shredded plant fiber and biological material is often more absorbent than other kinds, though different substrates retain humidity at different levels. Aspen bedding is one of the more commonly used plant substrates. It is cheap but is probably the driest of these options. Aspen bedding is considered controversial in many Ball Python and herpetological communities, in part, for this reason. Any substrate made up of large chunks like aspen bedding, cypress mulch, orchid bark, or shredded paper can also increase the risk of accidental ingestion. If your Ball Python does swallow a small amount of substrate, odds are it'll be fine, though in some cases, these kinds of substrates have been known to get lodged in the mouths of reptiles or even cause impaction.

If you plan on feeding your Ball Python in its main enclosure, remain vigilant of any discomfort or changes in behavior after feeding. For example, persistent yawning may be your snake's way of trying to dislodge a stuck piece of bedding.

Cypress mulch is another popular option for Ball Pythons. It is made from the bark of cypress trees and is a more natural-looking bedding. It is also relatively inexpensive, but, like aspen bedding, it can be messy and may need to be changed more frequently. Coconut husk is also a good option. It's natural and biodegradable, safe for the snake, and easy to clean, but it's also more expensive than some of the other options. One perk to coconut-based substrates is that they are less susceptible to growing mold due to their antimicrobial and antibacterial properties.

Another option is paper-based bedding, like newspaper, cage liners, or paper towels. This kind of bedding has the lowest risk of impaction, though it is the least natural looking and is often considered the least aesthetically pleasing substrate. Paper-based bedding is among the easiest substrates to clean, though it does almost nothing for humidity retention. It's cheap and easy to find.

Bioactive substrates and coconut soil have textures much closer to natural dirt. For this reason, they can be some of the best at retaining humidity as well as adding a natural look to your enclosure. They can be more difficult to clean, though, and are generally on the more expensive side. Coconut soil has the same antimicrobial properties as coconut husk.

Some substrates are not suitable for Ball Pythons and should be avoided. Cedar mulch and pine mulch have oils that can be toxic and irritating to reptiles. Sand can be easily swallowed, causing impaction, and can also be abrasive and irritating to scales, eyes, nostrils, and the mouth. Kitty litter or substrate marketed as "clumping" or "scoopable" may stick to your pet and can be highly hazardous if ingested. Artificial substrates like astroturf should also be avoided as they are difficult to clean, don't hold up to heat, and release potentially toxic chemicals over time.

More experienced owners may want a vivarium with living plants and a functioning micro-ecosystem. Bioactive substrate is your best option if this is your goal, as it can sustain plant life. UV lamps or sunlight would also be necessary for this kind of setup. Many owners with more elaborate setups like this often like to include backgrounds to give their tank additional aesthetic appeal and potentially make snakes feel more secure. A wide variety of backgrounds can be purchased from most pet stores or bought online. You can also create your own background with spray foam or other nontoxic materials.

Furnishings and decor are important for Ball Pythons for many of the same reasons as they're important for humans. All thinking creatures will benefit from some sort of mental stimulation and interesting surroundings. As mentioned earlier, the range of setups for Ball Pythons is vast. Many owners feel that their Ball Pythons benefit by having an enclosure that replicates the conditions of their natural habitat. The research seems to support this.

Studies have shown Ball Pythons display fewer atypical

Ball Pythons require their enclosure to maintain a specific humidity for optimal health. Generally, the ideal humidity for a Ball Python enclosure is between 60 and 70 percent. If the humidity in your snake's habitat is too low, your pet may have issues with shedding. Conversely, if the humidity is too high, your pet may be at increased risk for infection or scale rot. Humidity can be modified with water, ventilation, substrate, and misting. A hygrometer is a great way to measure humidity daily.

behaviors when housed in larger, better-furnished enclosures than when in more plain and barren enclosures. Having two hides, one for the warm side and one for the cool, is ideal. You can purchase reptile hides at most pet and feed stores in a variety of sizes and designs. You can also improvise certain items, like shoeboxes or overturned containers, for a temporary hide. Be aware that these will likely not fulfill your pet's needs as well or for as long. A proper hide is covered on all sides with a large enough opening and interior space that your Ball Python can enter and exit safely without getting stuck.

A water bowl is, of course, also necessary. You want to ensure that your water bowl is big enough for your Ball Python to partially soak in. Be careful choosing an overly large water bowl for hatchlings or juveniles, though, as they may struggle to get out if they fall in. A larger water bowl will help you keep a persistent source of humidity in your enclosure. You should change your snake's water every one to three days at a minimum.

Additionally, you may also want vertical structures for your Ball Python to climb and a few decorative logs or rocks to add some variety to the terrain. Any decorations should be safe for your snake to crawl over and should not add too much difficulty to how easily the reptile can move around the enclosure.

Setting up a safe heat source and thermostat

Once you have the enclosure, making sure it's properly heated is one of the biggest next steps. A warm spot in the enclosure should be between 90°F and 95°F, and the cooler side should be around 75°F to 80°F. This level of variety may allow your Ball Python to better thermo-regulate for its comfort and can incentivize the snake to be more active. Heating pads, basking lamps, ceramic heaters, radial heating panels, and heat tape are some of the most common devices owners use to supply additional heat.

As opposed to some other reptiles, Ball Pythons do not tend to bask in the sunlight in the wild for extended periods of time. Many sources say that, given a proper diet, they do not need sunlight to produce any additional vitamins. However, a UVB light source can allow your snake to adhere to a more natural day-night cycle, and some owners also claim that UVB light helps boost their snake's immune function. High-intensity light and UVB rays can be highly damaging for albino Ball Pythons,

Photo Courtesy of Courtney Hart

though. Their lack of pigment makes them much more suscep-tible to UV radiation damage to their eyes and scales. Many Ball Pythons may also be more hesi-tant to be active in their enclosure while exposed to bright light. If you incorporate any sort of bright or UV light system in your enclo-sure, be sure to turn it off in the evenings and at night while your snake is most active. Doing other-wise can upset the reptile's natural clock and cause the animal unnec-essary stress.

Buying a thermostat that you can plug your heat pad into directly is a necessity. Some heat pads can get over 130°F. Temperatures this high can severely burn your snake's belly. High temperatures from other sources can similarly cause burns or allow your snake to overheat if not monitored. For most thermostats, you should place the probe rest-ing directly on top of the heat pad strapped to the underside of your enclosure. Again, for the hot side of your tank, you'll want to set your thermostat to about 90°F. Heat pads will have trouble penetrating too thick a substrate, so be sure to consider this when deciding on the sub-strate or heat source so that you can plan accordingly.

Providing proper ventilation and humidity

In their natural habitat, Ball Pythons are subjected to a wide range of humidity levels throughout the year. As a result, they regularly move and adjust their surroundings when necessary. While capable of weathering too high or too low humidity for short periods, prolonged exposure to the extremes can cause deleterious effects to their health. In captivity, Ball Pythons do not have the ability to travel, and they rely on us to ensure that conditions are kept at ideal levels. Air flow and ventilation in homes are not subject to all the same forces as they are outside; therefore, we need to take these factors into account. Heat lamps, ceramic heaters, screen lids, ventilation holes, and the overall setup of your tank can also decrease humidity at rapid rates.

Captive Ball Pythons thrive in humidity levels of about 55 to 65%. Your average home is likely to have a humidity level between 35 and 45%, so adding additional moisture to your pet's enclosure is usually necessary for its health and proper shedding. You may even want to increase humidity levels higher, closer to 70 to 80%, when your snake is shedding, especially if it's having a difficult shed.

Many owners mist their pythons' enclosures with a spray bottle full of water when necessary. Checking humidity levels is the best way to determine how often your enclosure needs misting, but many owners will be within a safe range by misting one or two times a day. Observe and be aware of the moisture level in the tank while doing this. You don't want the tank to appear wet or dripping. Automatic misting systems are an available option, but these aren't generally necessary for the level of moisture that Ball Pythons need and can oversaturate your enclosure if not properly monitored.

Overly high humidity can result in the growth of fungus and mold, as well as cause bacterial infections of your snake's skin and respiratory system, especially within the enclosed and relatively unventilated space of your terrarium. You can purchase a hygrometer or a thermometer with humidity measuring capabilities if you want to be aware of the exact moisture level in your snake's enclosure.

If daily misting is not possible or ideal in your situation, you can also place a small container full of damp water-retaining materials like sphagnum moss or cypress mulch in your enclosure. Using a snake hide or an improvised container, your snake can freely self-regulate between humid and dry environments depending on its needs at the moment. Make sure the box is made of a safe material for your Ball Python, is water resistant, and cannot grow mold. Additionally, ensure that the container does not have sharp corners, straps, or anything that could otherwise injure or entangle your snake.

Cleaning Your Enclosure

Routine habitat cleaning, sanitizing, and maintenance

> *Weekly care mostly involves feeding, changing water, checking temperature and humidity, and misting or adding water to the substrate as needed. Spot cleaning when the snake defecates is another weekly job. The substrate can be completely changed out as needed, with the frequency depending on the individual snake, the type of substrate, and the size of the enclosure.*
>
> GARRICK DEMEYER
> *Royal Constrictor Designs*

Cleaning a glass tank, PVC cage, or plastic tub for a Ball Python is a relatively simple process, but one that you must do regularly to ensure the health and well-being of your snake. The first step is to remove the snake from the enclosure and place it in a safe and secure location. This is also a good time to check for any signs of illness or injury, such as mites or wounds.

You should start by removing and disposing of any substrate, such as aspen shavings or coconut fiber. Clean the bottom and sides of the tank using warm water with a small amount of dish soap. Use a scrub brush

or sponge to remove any clinging debris, remaining substrate, feces, or mystery stains. After the enclosure looks clean, use a mild or diluted disinfectant to sanitize the inside. A bleach solution and diluted white vinegar are two common household disinfectants that are effective and safe to use for your snake.

For bleach, you want to add at least nine parts water or more for every one part bleach. A mixture made of equal parts white vinegar and water is equally effective. For enclosures that you cannot easily move, use a spray bottle to mist the solution onto the surface and let it sit for 10 minutes.

You can also use veterinary-grade disinfectants like F10, so long as you very carefully follow all instructions. Using an undiluted solution or not following directions properly for some products may cause serious harm or even death in pets. There is a wide range of commercial products designed to sanitize your tanks as well. Each one touts its own benefits and uses, and each may have its own individual level of success. If you choose to buy a commercial formula to clean your enclosure, be sure to do enough research so that you feel confident in the product's safety.

Once the enclosure is sanitized, rinse the surface with water to remove any disinfectant. You can often smell if any disinfectants remain. If the surface or object still smells of disinfectant, additional rinses are recommended.

Once all glass is thoroughly cleaned and sanitized, dry it with clean rags, towels, or paper towels. Allowing your tank to drip dry is also an option, but this will take much longer, may not leave the tank as dry, and requires you to flip your tank upside down. Depending on the size of your tank, this may not be a good option as the weight and slipperiness of your tank could easily cause you to drop and potentially damage it. Make sure your tank is thoroughly dry by the end of this process, as a wet tank may create more humidity than you desire in your enclosure or expose your pet to potentially unsafe levels of cleaning solution.

You will also need to clean the water bowl, hide box, screen top, and any other accessories. Similarly, scrub these items with soap and water to remove any visible debris or stains, sanitize, and rinse them thoroughly before drying them.

Finally, you can add new substrate and accessories back into the enclosure and return your snake to its home. Make sure to keep an eye on your snake and monitor its health and repeat this cleaning process at least once a month. It's important to note that if you are using a heat or UV source, you should unplug or turn off the source before cleaning the enclosure and keep any plugs, wires, or electrical components from getting wet.

Consequences of inadequate care or poor enclosure quality

Inadequate care and poor enclosure quality can have significant consequences for the health and well-being of Ball Pythons. These snakes are very sensitive to their environment, and even small changes can cause stress and lead to a variety of health problems. One of the most common consequences of poor enclosure quality is an increased risk of infections, like scale rot, which can be difficult to treat and can become life-threatening. Poor ventilation and high humidity levels in the enclosure can also cause respiratory problems such as pneumonia, which can be fatal if not treated promptly.

Poorly designed or maintained enclosures can also lead to abnormal behavior patterns, such as lethargy, hiding, or aggression, and can negatively impact the snake's mental health. Additionally, Ball Pythons require specific temperatures and humidity levels to maintain a healthy appetite and digestion. Inadequate conditions can result in malnutrition, leading to stunted growth, weakened immune systems, and a decreased life span. To avoid these negative consequences, it is essential for owners to provide proper care and appropriate housing for their Ball Pythons.

CHAPTER 4

Caring for Your Ball Python

Feeding Your Ball Python

Choosing the right type and size of prey

> *This is just my opinion, but if they are available where you live, I prefer to feed my Ball Pythons natal multimammate rats—often called African soft furs—as opposed to the traditional Norway rats that many choose to feed their Balls. While all rats offer nutrition that will work, I feel like it's the difference between serving hamburger meat and filet mignon! Mice, on the other hand, should be avoided altogether for Ball Pythons.*
>
> BRIAN CARTER
>
> *BC's Balls*

Though Ball Pythons may not eat as often as many other kinds of pets, feeding is still something you will have to dedicate thought, time, and resources to as an owner. For some pythons and owners, there will be more struggle and learning needed than for others. There are a number of rules and considerations to follow that can help ease this process for first-time owners. Below, Jessica Collins of JC Pythons gives some great tips on determining the proper-size prey for your Ball Python.

"Be aware of the size of the prey item you're feeding your snakes. They naturally handle prey items two to three times the width of their head without problems. The general rule is to feed prey items roughly as wide as the widest part of the individual. If the prey item is too big, the snake won't eat."

Some Ball Pythons may attempt to eat oversized prey. If a Ball Python eats prey that is too large, then it may not be able to digest the meal before it starts to decompose. At that point, your Ball Python is likely to vomit, which causes distress and the potential for more harm to the snake. This should be avoided at all costs.

Ball Pythons have a reputation as picky eaters among hobbyist communities. Some snakes may only eat prey of a certain color, size, or species. For example, it's not uncommon for Ball Pythons that are started on mice as hatchlings to refuse to eat anything other than mice throughout their lives. As opposed to rats, mice are far less nutritious. Therefore, starting your Ball Python off on mice may not be ideal. If you've got a mouser on your hands, it's generally recommended to try and switch the snake over to rats if possible. Many Ball Pythons will make the switch, while others may stay stubborn indefinitely.

For more open-minded Ball Pythons, there's a wide range of potential prey animals that you can use to add some variety to their diet. The common Norway rat, chicks, quail hatchlings, young guinea pigs, young rabbits, gerbils, hamsters, and African soft fur rats are some of the additional items that owners have put on their snake menus. It's important

to note that many of these options will be more expensive than your typical rat.

Each prey item has its own unique considerations and nutritional makeup to take into account as well. For instance, I've heard stories of live hamsters killing Ball Pythons. Generally, these rodents can be more aggressive and territorial than other animals on the list. For this reason, hamsters are one animal I make a point to avoid feeding my Ball Python. African soft furs and gerbils, in particular, have gained loyal followings as these are animals much more likely to live in the Ball Python's native range and are said to have greater nutritional benefits.

I don't have any experience with African soft furs personally, but many owners and breeders speak highly of them as a food source. Brian Carter of BC's Balls, for example, describes African soft furs as a cut above other prey.

"This is opinion, but if you live where they are available, I prefer to feed natal multimammate rats, often called African soft furs, as opposed to the traditional Norway rats many owners feed their snakes. While rats offer nutrition that will work, it's like comparing hamburger meat to a filet mignon. Mice should be avoided altogether for Ball Pythons."

Growing up, all the Ball Pythons I had were fed live prey. For the first few years I had Saoirse, this is how I fed her because it was what she was used to. Saoirse had a tendency toward nervousness with live rats though. She would go from rigid and ready to strike to cowering in the corner if a particularly brazen rat ended up approaching or touching her. In one instance, Saoirse did not get a good grasp on her prey, only grabbing its back legs. As a result, it managed to reach around and bite her. I had to grasp the rat's neck myself to prevent it from doing further damage.

After that, I swore off live feeding. I immediately began researching the best options for getting dead prey. I found a local supplier of frozen rats in my area and began purchasing rats from them. Thankfully, Saoirse made the switch easily. She mostly did not hesitate to eat thawed rats. All things considered, she's probably much more comfortable eating prey that can't bite back.

Buying frozen rats in large quantities ended up saving me a lot of money compared with feeding live. Live rats cost me about $8 per rat, and buying frozen rats in packs of 10 or 15 cost me about $2 to $3 per rat. So, if you've got the extra freezer space and don't mind little pink eyes watching you every time you sneak a pint of ice cream late at night, storing frozen rats can be a good solution for those looking to save money. Though if you do not live near a supplier selling frozen rats, then you may have to pay for refrigerated shipping. I found a supplier about 30 minutes from my house, and I found the drive to be well worth it.

Buying frozen also guarantees that you know exactly where you'll be getting your Ball Python's next meal from, and you can plan with that assurance in mind. When buying live rats from my local feed store, there were occasionally periods of time where certain sizes of rats were hard to come by, as opposed to frozen rats, which you can typically buy in bulk.

To thaw your rats, simply remove one from the package and place it in some sort of waterproof packaging, such as a Ziploc bag. You can either let your rats thaw in your refrigerator overnight or you can soak the bag containing the rat in warm water for a minimum of 30 minutes. A soaked or cold rat may not appear as appetizing to your snake, though some do not mind. Be sure the prey is fully thawed though; partially frozen rats can make digestion more difficult and could present a serious hazard to your pet.

Although Ball Pythons are nonvenomous and generally docile, they have quite a few teeth! Ball Pythons have around 150 teeth, each measuring approximately one centimeter long. These teeth are shaped like tiny hooks and are designed to hold prey in place while the snakes go in for the kill. Unlike venomous snakes, Ball Pythons kill their prey by constriction and eventual suffocation.

Photo Courtesy of Michele Zurita

If buying pre-killed frozen rats isn't possible for some reason, but you don't want to feed your snake live prey, you can also buy live rodents and then kill them yourself. This situation isn't ideal for many owners, due to the stress or difficulty involved in killing the animal, though some manage without too much difficulty. Some of the most effective ways of doing this are enclosing the rat in an air-tight container and exposing it to high levels of carbon dioxide via a baking soda and vinegar mixture, dry ice, or other methods. Cervical dislocation is another quick and relatively painless way to quickly dispatch rodents. While using one hand or a rod to hold down the base of a rat or mouse's skull, use your other hand to yank the tail backward and upward. If done correctly, this will disconnect the animal's spinal cord from the brain, killing the rat instantly. This method may not be effective and shouldn't be performed on larger rats.

You should wear gloves if using a hands-on method to kill rodents. Killing prey yourself will significantly increase your chance of getting bitten, and without the skills and equipment to carry out these procedures correctly, you risk causing severe suffering to the animal. Avoid taking this route if other options are available and you're not a qualified professional.

Feeding frequency and prey size

In addition to larger prey, Ball Pythons will require less frequent feedings as they get older. Hatchlings eat much more often than older snakes; you will likely see your snake's metabolism gradually slow as it ages. If you only have smaller prey available, then you may need to give your Ball Python multiple animals in one feeding. As there can be significant variation between Ball Pythons in size and rate of growth, dietary needs for your Ball Python can be different from the needs of others. As stated earlier, prey should ideally be slightly slimmer than your snake's widest point. You can get a good idea of how much to feed your snake based on its age and weight as well.

Ball Python Age:	Hatchling (50–150g)	Juvenile (200–700g)	Adult (900–1800g+)
Size of prey:	Rat pinkies (5–10g)	Rat pups to small rats (15–50g)	Medium to large rats (80–150g+)
Feeding frequency:	Every 5–7 days	Every 10–14 days	Every 14–21 days

Your snake's behavior should also help give you a clue as to whether it's hungry. Your Ball Python will likely become more active and exploratory when it gets hungry.

Feeding tips and safety (separate feeding enclosure)

> *Many Ball Pythons will take rodents that have been frozen and thawed, though it is extremely important that the rodents are heated really well before being offered. Ball Pythons hunt primarily by scent and by the thermal signature given off by their prey, and a rodent that is room temperature is often not seen as food. But if the rodent is heated up to the correct temperature range, the snake will likely grab, constrict, and consume it just as if it were alive.*
>
> GARRICK DEMEYER
> *Royal Constrictor Designs*

Feeding your Ball Python typically presents few real threats, though you always run the risk of getting bitten, whether it be by the prey or your pet. There are snake hooks which you can use instead if you feel uncomfortable handling your snake during feeding. One point of major contention among Ball Python owners is whether or not to feed their snakes in an enclosure separate from the one that the snakes live in. In the past, conventional wisdom held that snakes enter "feeding mode" or "predator mode" whenever they see hands enter their tank. To avoid any mistake strikes or bites, owners would place their snakes in a separate enclosure when it was time to eat. Today, many people challenge the idea that Ball Pythons need to be fed in separate enclosures or that such a feeding mode exists. They often argue that being out of their typical space may stress the snake to the point of not eating or that handling the snake after it has eaten can cause it to vomit.

I have always used a separate enclosure to feed my Ball Pythons. While I think the concerns are legitimate, I have heard stories describing how their snakes became aggressive from enclosure feeding. I've never had a snake vomit after moving it from the feeding tub, and I have only ever been bitten while my snake was in said tub. When attempting to switch Saoirse over from live rats to thawed frozen ones, she once refused a meal. While removing the rat, I made the mistake of reaching my hand down right in front of her. I can only assume that she was still in predator mode despite not seeing the rat as fit for her refined palette. So instead, she struck at the more obviously warm, moving, and living thing moving toward her. Her teeth sinking into my hand was far more shocking than painful and the second she realized what she had done, she released me and shrank back into her tub.

From that moment onward, I was much more aware and purposeful when handling Saoirse, especially while she was in her feeding tub. I never had another incident after that.

For my feeding setup, I always use a plain plastic tub without any furnishings or bedding, as I remove my snakes immediately after they eat. The lack of bedding guarantees that your pet does not swallow any substrate and become impacted. After thawing a rat and washing my hands to remove any smell, I place my Ball

Python in her feeding tub. Using a pair of long feeding forceps, I pick up the rat by the hips. This keeps the rat far from my hands and keeps any scent from getting on me. I bring it down to about eye level with the snake and gently bounce and shake it in place to trick her into thinking it's alive. She usually strikes within a few seconds, but sometimes it takes a few minutes of coaxing. After that,

I usually wait a few minutes for her to get settled, then pick her up from behind and gently place her back into her enclosure in front of her hide.

Many owners may still find that using one enclosure for feeding and living is what works best for them and their snake. Setting up a separate feeding enclosure that your snake can spend one to three days in is also an option. Whatever setup you're using, it is best to minimize handling and contact for a few days after your snake has eaten.

Handling and Bonding with Your Ball Python

Approaching and handling your snake safely

> **"**
>
> *Handling should only happen after your new Ball Python is well acclimated and feeding regularly. Slowly introduce handling for 10 to 15 minutes at a time, and never handle the snake for pleasure 24 hours before or 48 hours after feeding because of the risk of causing regurgitation.*
>
> BRIAN CARTER
> *BC's Balls*
>
> **"**

Photo Courtesy of Dan Ferreira

Ball Pythons are not likely to be aggressive, though mishandling or mistakes can lead to bites. As described earlier, snakes may mistakenly strike if you put your hands near them while they're in feeding mode. They are likely to immediately let go once they realize you're not prey. Approaching your snake calmly and confidently is key. It's important to recognize that the snake has far more reason to be afraid of you than you do of it.

Avoid reaching for or making any jabbing motions toward the snake's head. These actions may trigger a fear response from your Ball Python. Anything quickly coming down toward it in that way may be seen as a predator. When holding your Ball Python, make sure you support the bulk of its weight and do not let the snake hang or dangle too much. Washing your hands before and after you handle your snake is a must. You don't want to expose the reptile to any irritating oils or scents, and you don't want to potentially spread any pathogens either from the snake or to it.

Bobby Tyler from RepTyler Ball Pythons gave some fantastic advice on how to handle your Ball Python around feeding time and in general.

"Handling, for the most part, is simple. Ball Pythons rarely choose to bite. When they do, it is always a feed response or a fear response. Learn to recognize the feeding behaviors and avoid trying to reach in and pick them up when they are in feeding mode. If they are in this mode, a simple touch to the head with a snake hook or other object is usually enough to let them know it's not feeding time. Always pick them up from behind simply because it's less threatening to the snake and is less likely to cause defensive behaviors. A quick, confident reach in and pick up is better than looming over them tentatively. This is more likely to result in defensive behavior, as is staring at the snake."

Bonding with your snake through regular handling and interaction

> *If you enjoy holding your Ball Python, do not handle it for several days after feeding. When taking your snake out, don't be nervous—your snake will know that you are afraid. Confidently open the enclosure and don't rush the snake—let the snake come to you! When you hold it, be sure you are supporting the whole body, so the snake feels secure, and remember that most pythons do not enjoy being touched on the head.*
>
> TOM HARBIN
> *Tom Harbin's Reptiles*

Photo Courtesy of
Arlen Chamberlain
Misfitballpythons

Ball Pythons, like any other animal, require regular handling and attention to better acclimate to your presence. Ball Pythons who are mostly left alone may be more skittish or more uncomfortable being handled. Frequent aggressiveness in unsocialized Ball Pythons is still uncommon, though not unheard of.

Holding your snake in your hands or letting it wrap around your arms is the primary way to get it used to human contact. Your natural body heat may feel very comfortable for your Ball Python. It may be content to just sit on you or stay wrapped around you for extended periods of time. Other snakes may be much more focused on slithering to freedom while being handled and will essentially use you as a human treadmill as you pass them from one arm to the other. It all depends on the personality of your snake and the animal's mood in that moment. Either way, this sort of contact will help build trust and familiarity between you and your Ball Python. At the same time, you must be aware that Ball Pythons are not social animals, and over-handling can lead to unnecessary stress. Handling a snake one to three times a week for roughly 20-minute intervals is a good balance that will help keep your pet comfortable while also ensuring that it acclimates to human touch.

Dealing with common behavior issues, such as striking or musking

As stated earlier, aggression is rarely a big problem among Ball Pythons. If you're worried your snake may strike, then ensure that any attempts at handling are initiated from behind. Also, using a snake hook or similar object to touch the snake may help quell aggression. If your snake is actively striking, that's a good sign that it doesn't want to be handled in that moment. The best thing to do is leave it alone in its enclosure and let it relax for a day or two before trying to handle it again.

Some Ball Pythons may emit a strong odor when being handled. This is called musking and is a sign that your snake is stressed or feels threatened. If your snake is doing this and exhibiting other signs of fear or aggression, then it is often best to leave it alone for a while. Strong smells can also be a sign that something is wrong with the health of your snake. If a Ball Python starts emitting unusual smells consistently, then be sure to look at the reptile thoroughly for any signs of illness and ensure that there aren't any feces or decaying matter within the enclosure.

Enrichment activities for your snake

Enrichment is an important part of keeping your Ball Python happy and healthy. Though Ball Pythons aren't particularly active and tend to be creatures of habit, they still need regular activities and obstacles to help keep them on their toes, figuratively. Taking your snake outside or letting it explore parts of your house is one great way to satiate any wanderlust your pet may be feeling. While doing this, it's vital that your snake does not escape or harm itself in any way.

Snakes must be watched closely, as they may try to escape into tight spaces or hard-to-reach areas. While outside, it's also very important to be very aware of other animals, like birds of prey, other pets, or even insects like ants. These creatures can all cause harm or even kill your Ball Python under the wrong circumstances.

Providing vertical decor and structure within your snake's enclosure is one way to help keep it entertained and let it burn some energy. Occasionally rearranging parts of your enclosure's decor may add some novelty and mental stimulation, though you want to largely leave the enclosure in the state to which the snake is acclimated.

Health and Hygiene

Signs of a healthy snake/Common health issues and how to spot and prevent them

When it comes to determining the health of a Ball Python, there are several key signs to look for. A healthy Ball Python will have smooth and shiny scales, with no signs of discoloration or abnormal shedding. The eyes should be bright and clear, with no discharge or cloudy appearance, apart from when the snake is beginning to shed. Any dark patches or stains on the snake's underside or elsewhere can be a sign of scale rot or other infections.

A healthy Ball Python should also have a strong appetite and should be eating regularly for its age. While hunger strikes are not uncommon, especially during the winter or when females are gravid, repeated or frequent fasting can be a sign of underlying health issues. The python should be able to easily digest food and have solid bowel movements and no regurgitation. The snake should be able to move freely and easily, with no signs of stiffness or lethargy.

The snake's nostrils and mouth should be free of excess fluid or dripping spittle or bubbles. When content and healthy, Ball Pythons are largely silent. Any wheezing, whistling, or abnormal noises could be a sign of respiratory infection or labored breathing.

It's important to monitor the snake's weight. The animal should be neither too thin nor too fat; these can be indicators of underlying health issues or improper care. Pythons should have a well-rounded body shape with good muscle tone and no irregular lumps or bumps, with a visible spine but not too pronounced. In addition to these signs, it's important to keep in mind your Ball Python's typical behavior. Changes in behavior or activity levels can indicate that something is not right with your snake. It is important to consult with a veterinarian who is experienced with reptiles if you have any concerns about the health of your Ball Python, or if you notice any of these signs.

Shedding guide and tips

Another important sign of a healthy Ball Python is a proper shedding cycle. Ball Pythons ideally shed their skin in one piece, starting at the head and working their way down the body. A healthy young snake will shed its skin every three to four weeks, while an older one may shed closer to every six to eight weeks. The skin should come off in one large piece, though a few breaks or little bits of stuck skin are not uncommon.

Humidity is a big part of how Ball Pythons maintain a healthy shed. If your snake is having trouble shedding or is inconsistent and patchy, then too-low humidity is often to blame. Consider elevating your enclosure's humidity levels while your snake is shedding if you notice any of these problems. Additionally, an occasional soak in warm water can help your Ball Python slough off any difficult skin and have a healthier shed. Be careful not to overdo it or get your snake's head underwater, as this can cause other issues, such as respiratory infections.

Before and After Shedding

Importance of regular check-ups and visits to the veterinarian

Just like any other animal, Ball Pythons are susceptible to a variety of health problems, and regular check-ups can help catch these problems early on before they become more serious. During a check-up, your veterinarian will examine your Ball Python to make sure that it is growing and developing normally and will check for any signs of illness or disease.

It is important to regularly take your Ball Python to the vet for check-ups and visits for several reasons. To start, your Ball Python may be experiencing health issues that are not easily visible to the naked eye. Health problems that go unnoticed for long periods of time can seriously impact the health of your pet, even threatening its life. A vet can perform a full examination and perform any necessary tests to ensure that your Ball Python is healthy.

Additionally, regular check-ups can help you catch any potential health problems early on. This allows you to address the issue before it becomes more serious and potentially life-threatening. Early treatment is always more effective and less expensive, so it is important to catch health problems early.

Another important reason to take your Ball Python to the vet regularly is to monitor its growth and development. Ball Pythons grow rapidly during the first few years of their lives, and it is important to ensure that they are growing and developing properly. Your vet can monitor your pet's growth and offer advice on how to best care for the snake, such as adjusting its diet or environment. By catching health problems early, monitoring growth and development, and receiving professional advice, you can ensure that your Ball Python lives a long and healthy life.

CHAPTER 5

Common Health Issues and Emergencies

Preventive Care

Implementing a regular health check-up routine

> *I recommend keeping a record of your python's weight, bowel movements, and shed cycles, as well as what it eats and how often. That way, you will have that information in hand in case of a veterinarian visit. Changes can happen quickly, and for an animal that doesn't eat daily, it can sometimes be difficult to remember the last time a bowel movement happened or when the snake last skipped a few meals.*
>
> JESSICA COLLINS
>
> *JC Pythons*

When in doubt, a check-up with a reputable reptile vet is the best way to either quell or confirm any concerns you may have. Many reptile experts recommend you bring your Ball Python

Photo Courtesy of
Jessica Pratt

in at least two times a year. Routine check-ups are a great way to gauge the quality of your care and your pet's health. These appointments are also vital for catching health problems early and addressing emerging issues. It is wise to request a fecal examination along with your snake's check-up to get a more holistic picture of your Ball Python's well-being.

The vet will likely check your snake for any parasites, record its weight, and observe its overall condition. Feedback from the vet can be vital for improving the quality of your Ball Python's care and correcting any mistakes you may have made along the way. Online forums and herpetology Facebook groups may be able to direct you to trusted specialists in your area. Pet stores, feed stores, and local breeders can also be a fantastic resource for finding the right vet for you and your snake. A quick Google search and perusal of online reviews can also get you started in your vet search.

Administering preventive medications and treatments

You may have to wait up to several weeks to get an available appointment if a medical issue isn't serious enough to warrant a visit to an expensive emergency vet. In the meantime, some tried-and-true home

treatments can help keep your snake in stable condition and combat some common health problems with Ball Pythons.

For example, there are a variety of methods used to treat mild cases of scale rot at home. A diluted hypochlorous acid solution can help clean and clear the affected area. A diluted Betadine solution can also be used as a soak for your Ball Python. Betadine is a nonprescription antimicrobial. Applying Betadine directly can cause dryness and be irritating to your python, so it's recommended to instead mix about one part Betadine for every 10 parts warm water and let your Ball Python soak in it for about 20 minutes.

Make sure your Ball Python is secure in the container while soaking and can't escape. One way to do this is to use a large, lidded container or bucket that you can drill air holes in. Let the snake soak for about half an hour and keep checking the water temperature. Hot water can scald your snake, and cold water can send it into shock. Lukewarm water, about 85°F, comfortable to the touch, is ideal for soaking your Ball Python. Your snake can get even sicker if its head is submerged or if it is left unattended for too long in cold water. With any treatment option, be sure to handle your snake gently and watch it carefully throughout the process.

Mites and other endoparasites also have over-the-counter solutions designed to minimize symptoms and keep infection at bay. Pyrethroid insecticides, carbaryl powder or solution, Nix, and Provent-a-mite are some treatment options to consider when dealing with these issues. Be very cautious and follow all instructions to the letter when using these kinds of products, as they can be dangerous or even deadly to your snake if misused.

If you suspect that something is wrong with your Ball Python, it is essential that you schedule a vet visit as soon as possible. While some issues may be treatable at home, it's impossible to really know the scope of the illness without a proper examination. Not treated properly and swiftly, mild symptoms can progress rapidly or even return with a vengeance in snakes you believe were cured. At-home treatment should always be done in addition to a veterinary consultation or with the vet's instruction.

Common Health Issues

> If you notice mucus coming from the mouth, this can be a sign of a respiratory infection; this is by far the biggest issue with pythons in captivity. You'll also want to be on the lookout for any discolored scales, especially around the belly. This can be a sign of scale rot and is usually caused by substrate that is too wet, which allows bacteria to grow freely.
>
> BOBBY TYLER
> *RepTyler Ball Pythons*

Respiratory infections

In the wild, Ball Pythons spend much of their time in humidity-controlled burrows, so they can be sensitive to respiratory illness if they experience changes in temperature or humidity. It is important to monitor the humidity and temperature of your Ball Python's enclosure to ensure that it is within the optimal range for the snake's health. Respiratory illness can manifest as wheezing, whistling, or gurgling sounds that accompany breathing. Fluid or mucus discharge from the nose and mouth are also common manifestations of illness.

If you notice any of these symptoms, it is important to take your snake to a veterinarian as soon as possible for treatment. In severe cases, respiratory illness can lead to pneumonia and other serious complications. Proper care and attention to the environment of your Ball Python can help prevent respiratory illness and ensure that your snake stays healthy and happy.

Skin infections

It is important to regularly monitor your Ball Python's skin for any signs of infection, such as discoloration, swelling, or discharge. Ball Python scale rot is a common condition that occurs when the scales on a Ball Python's skin become infected or necrotic. It is usually caused by improper husbandry practices, such as keeping the snake in an enclosure that is too humid or dirty. Symptoms of scale rot include patches of dis-colored or missing scales, brown or raw- looking skin, numerous small, blister-like lesions that may be on the underside of the snake, or a foul smell. If left untreated, scale rot can lead to more seri-ous health issues, such as sepsis or organ failure.

To prevent scale rot, it is important to properly clean and maintain the snake's enclosure, provide appropriate humidity levels, and monitor the snake's

Scale rot is a relatively common problem for snakes. Various factors, including unsanitary living conditions, inappropriate humidity, and vitamin deficiencies, can cause this ailment. Symptoms of scale rot can include:

- Crusty scales or skin
- Skin discoloration
- Loss of appetite
- Swollen or raised scales

Mild scale rot may be treatable at home, but early medical attention can prevent serious illness. Don't hesitate to contact your vet and rule out any underlying conditions if your Ball Python develops scale rot symptoms.

overall health. If your snake is showing signs of scale rot, it is important to consult a veterinarian as soon as possible and begin trying some of the remedies discussed earlier to keep it from progressing.

Infectious stomatitis (Mouth rot)

Mouth rot is an infection caused by bacteria or fungi, often because of an unclean or improperly maintained enclosure. An untreated wound, malnutrition, or a weakened immune system can all also make your Ball Python more susceptible to mouth rot. Inflammation, drooling, a bad smell, and mouth breathing are all common signs of mouth rot. Mouth rot causes decreased appetite and discomfort in mild cases. Extreme cases result in sepsis and can be fatal. As with all other listed illnesses, you should contact your vet at the first signs of infection.

Egg binding

Egg binding is a condition that occurs when a female Ball Python is unable to pass her eggs naturally during the laying process. This can be caused by obesity, improper diet, or unsuitable nesting conditions. A diseased snake, one that's too young, too old, or has reproductive deformities, has a higher risk of egg binding. If a female Ball Python is experiencing egg binding, it is important to seek veterinary care as soon as possible. The veterinarian may be able to manually assist in the laying process or may recommend medical intervention such as calcium supplements or oxytocin injections. It is important to prevent egg binding by providing a healthy diet and proper care for your Ball Python, including access to a suitable nesting area and making sure your snake is in good enough condition to breed.

Septicemia

Septicemia occurs when bacteria enter the bloodstream of an animal. This can cause organ failure and eventually death. Septicemia is one of the worst diagnoses you can get as a pet owner. It often occurs in the late stages of infection when the snake is critically ill. At this stage, your Ball Python only has about a 50% chance of survival. Early detection and treatment with prescription-grade antibiotics are key to your snake's survival in these circumstances. Lethargy, lack of appetite, trouble breathing, and discoloration are some typical signs of septicemia. Infection from injury, improper care, parasites, and other illnesses can all result in this deadly infection. In most cases, a Ball Python in this condition needs immediate emergency care to survive.

Mites and parasites

> *If you ever come across mites on your snake, I find that the best way to take care of this is with olive oil. Traditional mite spray never seems to work all that well, and the mites always end up coming back. But when I've coated my snakes in olive oil, the mites get suffocated and die. I've found it also helps to leave the tank as bare as possible so mites don't have anywhere to lay their eggs.*
>
> JOANNA ALZATE-SHERKSNAS
>
> *CB Reptile*

Snake mites or *Ophionyssus natricis* are the most common parasite in the captive reptile trade. These arachnids are only visible as tiny black dots on your Ball Python's scales, especially concentrated around the ears, eyes, and vent. They bite reptiles, drinking their blood, which can cause the animals to lose their appetites and become lethargic. Skin irritation caused by mites may manifest as your snake rubbing and scratching itself against objects and soaking

for long periods. Prolonged infestations can lead to serious illness in your snake, up to anemia, septicemia, and even death.

Doing a deep clean of your enclosure and all items within, allowing it to soak with hot water and a few drops of dish soap, should be the first step you take in treating a mite infection. That, combined with a commercial-grade mite treatment, may be enough to clear up your mite issue. If the issue persists or is severe, then a visit to the vet is likely necessary.

Burns

Burns are a very common problem among Ball Pythons with unregulated or unmonitored heat setups. Heating pads can reach extremely high temperatures, causing the scales on your snake's belly to burn. Ball Pythons are generally pretty good about relocating if their current location doesn't meet their temperature needs. Some Ball Pythons without a thermometer-controlled heat source may go years without sustaining any kind of burns. A sudden appearance of burns could indicate other issues with your Ball Python's health that are changing its behavior. Burns, if untreated, can result in much more serious infections. A change in behavior and serious burns warrant a trip to the vet and adjustments to your enclosure's heat setup.

Emergencies

Recognizing the signs of an emergency

There are a number of signs that suggest something may be wrong with your Ball Python. As your Ball Python becomes acclimated to its enclosure, you should make a point to observe it. Getting to know the snake's daily habits allows you to be aware of sudden or drastic deviations from its normal behavior. Such changes can alert you to health problems or anything that may be making your snake uncomfortable or stressed.

Increased aggression, lethargy, and skittishness can point to potential problems with your Ball Python. Difficulty shedding or drastic changes in the frequency of shedding can also indicate illness or improper conditions in the enclosure. Changes in the texture, consistency, or frequency of your snake's feces can point to gastrointestinal issues. Discharge from your snake's eyes, nose, mouth, or any other orifice are often signs of infection.

If your Ball Python curves its neck and head upward and seemingly stares at the ceiling, this can be a sign of a serious neurological condition known as stargazing. Stargazing has causes rooted in a variety of potential illnesses and injuries. If your snake exhibits this or other odd or impaired motor functions, you should take it to a vet immediately.

Providing first aid and basic care

In a worst-case scenario where you might have to provide first aid to your Ball Python, it's important to be prepared. Having a small kit ready can make the difference and allow you to properly treat your snake in the event of an emergency. Betadine and triple-antibiotic ointments without analgesics are two great antimicrobial solutions to have on hand. Zero painkiller options of common brands like Neosporin are safe and effective on snake wounds. Cotton swabs and Q-Tips make good applicators for such ointments.

These are by no means long-term solutions and are only intended to stave off infection long enough for you to get your Ball Python to the vet. Overreliance or improper use of antibiotics can result in infections that are much harder to treat. If your snake is injured, remove any substrate that may become stuck in the wound. Remove any dirty materials or potential source of infection. It may be a good idea to move your snake to a clean and sterile spare enclosure entirely until the snake has a chance to be looked at.

Transporting the snake to the veterinarian

A cloth bag or inside-out pillowcase are some everyday items you can use to safely transport your snake. Be sure the opening is tied closed so your Ball Python does not get loose in your car. A small travel carrier lined with warm, comfortable material can also be suitable. Be sure your Ball Python cannot squeeze through, push open, or easily unlatch any container you use. Placing a blanket on top of your carrier can keep your snake warmer and help shield it from outside sights and smells. Make the trip as short as possible. Avoid unnecessary stops or high traffic hours if possible.

Working with the veterinarian to diagnose and treat the issue

Keeping logs of your Ball Python's diet, weight, and daily habits can be a major boon for the vet. Be prepared to describe any changes in behavior or any additional symptoms that your snake may have had leading up to the visit. The more information you can give the vet, the more likely they are to get to the root of your snake's problem quickly. Any changes in the snake's enclosure or lifestyle can help the vet determine what is causing these problems and better allow you to prevent them in the future. You should be receptive and open to your vet's judgments and conclusions in order to work toward the best possible solutions for your snake.

CHAPTER 6

Breeding Ball Pythons

Preparing for Breeding

When are Ball Pythons ready to mate?

Male Ball Pythons can technically reach sexual maturity as early as six months old, while females may be capable of reproducing at about one year. However, it is important to consider size, health, and other factors as well. Snakes that are capable of breeding may not yet be large enough or at the best point in their development to do so safely or easily. Female Ball Pythons are typically in the best shape to reproduce after three years or when they weigh about 1500 grams. Egg laying is taxing on female snakes, and they need to have adequate fat reserves to burn.

It is also important to make sure the male and female Ball Pythons are compatible, with no aggression present between them, and that the female is in good physical condition before attempting to breed them. If you have any doubts, seek the advice of a veterinarian or experienced breeder to ensure the breeding process is done safely and responsibly. When placed with a male, a receptive female Ball Python may expose pheromone glands and begin to sweep her tail back and forth to waft their scent into the air.

In the wild, Ball Pythons typically breed during the rainy season, from September to November. In captivity they aren't typically kept on a strict cycle, but lowering the temperature of your enclosure in the evenings

Ball Pythons Breeding

and lessening the number of daylight hours your snake is exposed to may help put your Ball Python in the right mood.

Selecting healthy and genetically diverse breeding pairs (and how to pair them)

If you decide to breed your Ball Python, it's best to know exactly what morph you've got and its genetic background. If you're not sure about your snake's genetics, genetic tests can be bought online. As discussed in Chapter Two, some morphs should not be bred together as they often produce offspring with genetic illnesses and defects. Other morphs and morph crosses are highly valued for their stunning visuals and unique appearance. If you're attempting to produce any specific morph, you will likely have to spend a great deal of time researching the genetic complex you have in mind and how your morph's genetics interact with the genetics of other morphs you're interested in crossing it with.

Other than the crazy world of Ball Python genetics, there are a few other factors to consider when deciding what snakes to pair together. Above all, ensuring that both snakes are healthy, a suitable age, and a good weight should be your top priority. When it comes time to try and breed them, just place both snakes together in the same enclosure. Two healthy snakes are usually able to figure out the rest. When pairing

two snakes, check to ensure neither of them is being aggressive toward the other.

Sexing the snakes

Before breeding two Ball Pythons, you first need to guarantee that you have a male and female snake. The easiest and most reliable way to do this is through a quick physical examination, often called sexing. When first deciding to sex your Ball Python, the first thing you may want to do is put on gloves. This is for the protection of your snake, as it acts as a preventative measure to keep you from possibly exposing the reptile to any germs you may be carrying on your hands. The gloves are also helpful in the off chance the snake decides to defecate or urinate during the probing process.

To sex a Ball Python, gently hold the snake and carefully examine its underside. You are looking for the presence or absence of a protrusion called the hemipenal bulge. This bulge is located just behind the vent, which is the opening at the base of the tail through which the snake excretes waste and eggs. The vent will appear as a slightly curved line along the width of the snake's tail. It is also flanked by two pelvic spurs, which are small, claw-like spikes on either side of the vent. Male Ball Pythons will usually have larger spurs than females. There are a few other physical indicators of sex in Ball Pythons that may give you some clues. Males tend to also be much smaller than females on average.

Male Ball Pythons have two hemipenal bulges, one on each side of the vent. Hemipenal bulges can be difficult to see in younger snakes or those that are not well-fed, so it may be necessary to gently manipulate the tail in order to get a good look. Female Ball Pythons do not have hemipenal bulges. Instead, they have a single, smooth area just behind the vent.

It is important to be gentle and careful when handling and examining your snake, as rough handling can cause stress and injury. It can be a good idea to have a veterinarian or experienced snake keeper help you with the process if you are unsure of what to look for. One way to confirm the presence of a hemipene is through a process known as popping. As scary as that might sound, your Ball Python should have no harm come to it if the process is done correctly. If done too roughly, though, popping can injure your snake.

Start by laying your Ball Python on a flat surface and flipping it over so the vent is exposed. Place one thumb just under the vent and the other just above it. Use the above thumb to gently try and open the vent by applying a small amount of pressure. Use the other thumb to press down below the vent. If done correctly, this method may cause a male python's hemipenes to pop out and be clearly visible. This will look like two red bumps or cylinders. The lack of this organ indicates that the Ball Python is female.

Another method to differentiate the sex of a Ball Python is a method called probing. You will need a probe, which is a thin, flexible rod with a rounded tip. First, make sure the snake is relaxed and not stressed, as this will make the process easier and safer for both you and the reptile.

Then, gently insert the probe into the snake's vent, which is the opening located at the base of the tail. If the probe goes in easily and meets resistance about two to three inches in, the Ball Python is likely a male. If the probe goes in easily and meets resistance four to six inches in, it is likely a female.

It's important to be gentle and use caution when probing a python, as the probe can cause injury if inserted too forcefully. It's also important to remember that probing is not a foolproof method for sexing pythons, and it's always best to consult with a veterinarian or experienced reptile keeper if you are unsure.

Setting up a breeding enclosure and providing appropriate conditions

Ball Pythons will require similar conditions while breeding as they do in their normal enclosures. Breeding can last several days, so while the snakes are getting at it, you need to make sure the conditions of their enclosure are conducive to their health and comfort. If a male Ball Python seems uninterested in mating, you can try adding another male Ball Python's shed skin to the breeding enclosure. If the snake perceives competition, then it may become much more motivated to hook up.

You can also add another male Ball Python into the enclosure for a brief period of time, though this comes with a high risk of aggressive behaviors between

A license is not required to own a Ball Python in most areas of the United States. However, owning any type of pet snake in Hawaii is illegal. Due to their non-aggressive nature and lack of venom, Ball Pythons are popular and low-maintenance pets. In contrast, venomous snakes are more likely to require a license due in part to the damage these animals could cause to the local ecosystem upon escape. Some states or counties may require a permit for snake ownership, so be sure to check with your local government before bringing home your new Ball Python.

the two if you're not controlling the situation. I would not recommend this method due to the added risks unless you're highly experienced in Ball Python breeding. If you do choose to introduce another snake, ensure that it's the same size as your other male and that you watch very closely. The new male may also breed with the female before your intended sire has the chance.

The Breeding Process

Locking behavior

When Ball Pythons are ready to mate, the male and female will twist their tails together and remain in this position anywhere from an hour to a few days. Some males will not lock as readily as others. This lack of interest can have a plethora of causes. Your male may not be large enough or mature enough, or either one of your snakes may be sick or unhealthy. Though you want to keep an eye on your Ball Pythons, you also want to give them adequate privacy, as they may be uncomfortable and unwilling to lock if they feel they're being watched.

Two Ball Pythons in "Lock"

Developing behavior

A pregnant female Ball Python will likely become less active and will prefer slightly cooler temperatures. It may also begin curling around its water dish regularly and begin to look lumpier due to the presence of growing follicles. The immature eggs, known as follicles, can be felt by palpating the lower two-thirds of your snake's body. Using the thumb and index finger, squeeze along the snake's body as it moves through your hands. The follicles will feel like speed bumps or beads nestled within the body cavity. If breeding was successful, the follicles will grow and will be easier to feel as time goes on.

The presence of follicles is confirmation that your snake has been bred. You can also determine how many eggs she will lay based on the number of follicles present. An ultrasound can also be used to display a female Ball Python's follicles. Female Ball Pythons may experience a change to the color of the scales or an increase in brightness and intensity. Your snake may also lie inverted or on its side more often, especially as the eggs grow. While your snake is gravid, it will likely refuse food until after it lays eggs.

Ovulation

Ovulation in Ball Pythons is different from ovulation in humans in that it occurs after breeding. A female snake can store sperm for months before it begins to ovulate and fertilizes its eggs. When ovulation begins,

Baby Ball Pythons are called "hatchlings."

the female Ball Python will start to swell rapidly, becoming much thicker and rounder. Three-fourths of her body will look majorly swollen. At this point, there's no mistaking that it's gravid. When this happens, the snake will be about 45 days away from laying eggs. Another sign of ovulation is a scrunched tail. This is a normal part of the process and is just body fat redistributing itself.

Pre-lay shed

A female Ball Python will typically shed about 15 days after it starts ovulating. It will be about 30 days out from laying eggs at this point. During any shed, your snake may benefit from additional humidity. While gravid, your snake may have trouble moving around and self-regulating, so increasing humidity to the enclosure's upper ranges may be beneficial. When it gets closer to laying eggs, your snake may begin to seek warmer temperatures. Prior to laying, the Ball Python may be restless, but it will likely begin to start coiling up in a comfortable, warm spot. Your female snake's spine may begin to protrude more, creating an upside-down V-shape.

Laying

Once your female has started laying eggs, it can take up to 12 hours for the process to finish, so patience is key. You should try and give your Ball Python privacy and minimize stress in this period. While laying, your snake may be a bit more defensive or aggressive than usual. If your snake seems to still be having trouble laying eggs after an extended period, you should contact a vet.

Moving, candling, and incubating eggs

Ball Pythons can lay anywhere from one to 15 leathery eggs in a brood. These eggs typically take between 50 and 65 days to hatch. It is not uncommon for some eggs to come out unfertilized; these are called slugs in the herpetology community. To remove the eggs, gently grasp the female at the back of the neck and tail and carefully uncurl the snake from its brood. Your Ball Python can be moved to a temporary enclosure while you move its eggs to an incubator, and then the snake can be moved back to its usual home.

Eggs should always be handled with extreme care. Normally, the eggs are laid stuck together. It is possible to separate many eggs, but you risk tearing them in the process. You should not separate eggs if they don't easily come apart. Separating eggs does make the spread of mold from egg to egg less likely, so there are a number of factors to take into account on whether or not to try and separate your clutch.

To check if an egg has been successfully fertilized, place a light source, like a flashlight, against the surface of the shell. Ensure all the other lights in the room are turned off. The rest of the egg will glow orange, and eggs with successfully developing embryos will appear veiny. Unfertilized eggs will be empty. About one week after the eggs are laid, they can accurately be tested with this method.

Avoid candling your eggs too frequently, as this can cause damage to the snakelet's developing eyes. It also requires you to frequently remove the eggs from their incubators, which interferes with temperature and humidity control. Once you've verified that your eggs are viable, many breeders recommend you don't disturb them until about a week before they hatch. Other breeders say it's acceptable to candle eggs about once a week to monitor their progress.

Ball Python eggs should be incubated between 88°F and 90°F at around 85% to 95% humidity. While eggs do well with high humidity, moisture, condensation, or standing water can jeopardize their viability.

After Breeding

Hatchling care

Ball Python hatchlings require intimate care to ensure they grow up to be healthy, happy snakes. Because they've received no prior human contact, some hatchlings may be skittish or prone to strike. This is nothing to worry about. With consistently gentle yet firm handling, the snakes should eventually become acclimated to you. Early development is a key period in establishing good behaviors in your Ball Python. Do not be afraid to handle slightly ornerier snakelets, as not doing so may prolong these negative behaviors.

It's important to strike an appropriate balance though. Like adults, baby Ball Pythons will become stressed with overhandling. Some breeders recommend giving them space and not unnecessarily handling them until their first shed. When it comes to feeding, hatchlings should be fed appropriately sized prey items, such as pinkie rats. If a hatchling refuses to eat pinkies, then it may eat hopper mice. Ball Pythons typically won't eat until about a week after their first shed. After that, they should be offered food every five to seven days.

Housing your hatchlings

Hatchlings require a similar setup to adults, with a few exceptions. An enclosure should be at least 10 gallons and should be equipped with a secure lid to prevent escape. The enclosure should be equipped with a suitable substrate, such as aspen shavings and paper towels. It should also provide a temperature gradient, with one end of the enclosure reaching a temperature of 85 to 90°F and the other end reaching 75 to 80°F. The enclosure should also have a hide box, which should be large enough for the hatchling to curl up inside. The hide box should be placed on the cooler side of the enclosure. A shallow water dish should also be provided.

First shed

Your Ball Python should shed for the first time at about two weeks old. Clutch mates should shed within a day or two of each other. Large discrepancies in your hatchlings' first shed could indicate low humidity or other concerns. Keeping your hatchlings on damp paper towels can help ensure an easy first shed. Many breeders will even continue to keep them in their incubators until their first shed, as long as conditions are suitable, and only then move them to their own enclosures. Hatchlings can enjoy their first meal about a week after their first shed.

Monitoring health and development

Any advice I could give on monitoring your baby Ball Python would not be much different than what has been recommended for adult Ball Pythons already. For the first week of the baby snake's life, give it a little extra space so it can get acclimated and begin to feel safe in its surroundings. Hatchlings have similar humidity and heating requirements as adults. So watch for burns, monitor temperatures, and make sure conditions are set up so that the snake can have a healthy first shed. As always, a difficult or patchy shed might suggest you need to up your humidity levels.

During the early stages of their lives, Ball Pythons grow rapidly. Regularly checking the length and weight of your young Ball Python can help you monitor its progress and ensure it's maturing at a healthy rate. Slow growth or little weight can indicate you need to feed your snake more frequently or switch it to larger prey. Make sure you schedule a vet visit for your growing Ball Python.

CHAPTER 7

Troubleshooting and Problem-Solving

Common Problems and Solutions

Dealing with picky eating and malnutrition

As discussed earlier, occasional hunger strikes and fasting are relatively common problems with Ball Pythons. These can occur as a natural response to the winter months, in preparation for laying eggs, inadequate conditions in their habitat, poor health, or for seemingly no reason at all.

Some Ball Pythons may prefer a specific kind of prey to others. When buying a Ball Python, you should inquire into the snake's diet in order to make the transition as easy as possible. Some snakes also have a strong preference for live prey over pre-killed, while others may be the opposite or have no preference. If you find yourself at a roadblock and your snake won't eat, you may need to start trying the range of available options. Some Ball Pythons may not be as picky

On average, Ball Pythons can live 20 to 30 years in captivity and around 10 years in the wild. The oldest documented Ball Python in captivity is a snake in the St. Louis zoo who was approximately 63 years old as of 2021. This Ball Python has not been named and has lived in this zoo since 1961. Another long-lived Ball Python lived to be 47 years old at the Philadelphia zoo.

as others. The only way to test this is to try and diversify their diets on occasion. Alternatively, maintaining a regular routine may help your Ball Python eat more consistently.

Switching out Norway rats for chicks or African Soft Furs should give you a good gauge on your snake's level of pickiness, and if successful, should allow your Ball Python to obtain a wider range of nutrients. In the wild, Ball Pythons will remain in one location, ambushing unsuspecting rodents until it becomes time to poop and shed. At this point, the area will repel most rodents because it has been thoroughly saturated with the Ball Python's scent. The Ball Python will then move on to a new location. By replicating the conditions of its natural habitat, you can try and engage the natural instincts that normally stimulate the snake's appetite. To recreate this process in captivity, you should thoroughly clean your Ball Python's enclosure, removing any scent or trace that might be lingering, especially if this is where you typically feed your snake. Introducing your snake to a new enclosure while it's eating may also work toward this goal.

A few days after your Ball Python sheds and you deep clean, you can then try introducing your Ball Python's preferred food. If your snake does not eat after all that and there are signs of weight loss or ill health, then you may need to consider the possibility of there being more serious causes for the snake's pickiness. Prolonged fasting for months and weight loss can be signs of a serious health problem and should be assessed by a vet.

There is a wide range of advice available for treating the problem of pickiness in Ball Pythons. Bill Crisp of K2C Wildlife Encounters, LLC recommends doing adequate research and establishing a routine to help a Ball Python maintain a consistent and healthy diet. *"Two things come to mind right off the bat: find a reliable and healthy food source from a good breeder or pet shop. Keep in mind what you feed. Diet is going to affect the health of your snake. So, feeding it food sources bought at a cheaper cost from a place that maybe doesn't keep up the cleaning of their mice and rats will impact your snake. So do research on rodent vendors—again, another good reason for going to a reptile expo. You can actually talk to the rodent breeders and see what they have available to buy. The other thing is the feeding schedule. With young Ball Pythons, feeding them every five to seven days is critical, especially at the beginning when they're young. Ensure you're not feeding them too much as they get older. Adult Ball Pythons should be eating every seven to 10 days, depending on the age of the snake; if it's an older, larger snake, it may only need to eat every 10 to 15 days."*

Handling aggression and fear in Ball Pythons

It's important to remember that Ball Pythons lack an amygdala—the part of the brain that processes emotion. Like most ectothermic animals, Ball Pythons lack the ability to feel happy, sad, angry, and so on. They are driven purely by instinct. If your Ball Python bites, it's not because you made it mad but because it felt threatened. Similarly, if it hugs around your arm or neck and stays there, it's not because it likes you, but because you're warm.

BRIAN CARTER

BC's Balls

For many owners, snake fear and aggression thankfully may not be common problems. Any bites that occur are more likely to have stemmed from a food response rather than a fear response, but there are always exceptions.

Ball Pythons, while generally docile, have their own complex personalities and experiences that inform their behaviors. Ball Pythons that have had bad past experiences or who have not received sufficient acclimation and socialization with humans may be more prone to strike. They may also just be jumpy or aggressive due to their genetics and individual personalities. Some Ball Pythons will have different baselines and limits for their outgoingness and tolerance for contact. With work and regular handling, you may be able to make them more comfortable and shift their behavior over time, but different Ball Pythons can end up having vastly different needs and outcomes when it comes to their sociability. In the end, it's best to be aware that these differences are out there and to try and ensure that you've got a good idea of what your Ball Python's personality is like before you buy it so that you can accommodate its needs to the best of your ability.

"I would be aware of how the animal behaves so you can best pick the one that fits into your life," says Jessica Collins of JC Pythons. *"Ball Pythons are not cats or dogs; their behaviors are different, but contrary to popular belief, individual snakes have personalities. I have animals in my collection that do*

not prefer to be handled. They hiss and strike and generally do not desire to be bothered. And there are animals in my collection that seemingly beg to be handled and are content with being held and passed around to visitors for hours without so much as a peep. And there is every snake personality in between. I'd be aware of how the animal behaves so that you can bring the best one into your home. If purchasing an animal online through a breeder, I would ask about the general personality of the animal you're purchasing."

Solving problems with the enclosure, such as humidity or temperature issues

While some issues may stem from your Ball Python, others can be caused by improper conditions in the enclosure. Problems with temperature and humidity can have a serious impact on your snake's health and behavior. Overly cold or hot environments can cause your snake to become lethargic, stressed, sick, or even fatally ill if not corrected quickly. Having a heating pad controlled by a thermometer ensures that you can adjust temperatures as needed so that your snake does not become sick or injured. Keep the enclosure away from windows or other sources of heat to keep your Ball Python from accidentally overheating.

If you have problems keeping the temperature in a suitable range, you might consider changing the kind of enclosure you keep your snake in. Plastic tubs or PVC enclosures will regulate temperatures much better than glass tanks, for example. Low humidity can be solved with regular misting, but high humidity can be just as harmful, if not more so. High humidity can foster bacterial growth and diseases like scale rot.

*Photo Courtesy of
Arlen Chamberlain
Misfitballpythons*

Changing the substrate in your snake's enclosure can help solve some humidity issues. Some substrates absorb and retain water better than others. Refer back to the chapter on substrates and enclosures for a more comprehensive list. The kind of enclosure you have also greatly affects humidity and temperature. Plastic tubs, for example, will retain humidity more than a glass terrarium. Ventilation ports and airflow will also greatly affect humidity.

Seeking Professional Help

Identifying when to seek the help of a veterinarian or reptile specialist

There are a large number of signs and symptoms that suggest something could be wrong with your Ball Python. Poor sheds, discoloration, prolonged dullness, dripping noses or bubbles around the mouth, weight loss, skittishness, and whistling breaths are some symptoms of common Ball Python illnesses and generally poor health.

Creating a regular routine and habitually examining your snake and its enclosure can give you a heads-up on any issues before they become advanced and can help prevent problems from occurring in the first place. Making cleanliness and vigilance a norm is ideal for staying on top of your Ball Python's health.

Bill Crisp of K2C Wildlife Encounters, LLC says, *"Keeping up with the enclosure throughout the week is preferred. Remove all waste to ensure you're not allowing the snake to slither or lie in its own feces. Changing out the water bowl daily is preferrable but can be done every other day. Checking the temperatures and humidity in your tank on a daily basis is very important, as is ensuring that your heat lamps and your heating pad are functioning to where the snake does not get cold. At least once a month—and some pet owners do it twice a month—take everything out of the enclosure, clean the enclosure with a bleach solution, and clean all the hides and decor that you have in the tank. Something you should do on a weekly basis is to inspect your snake, checking for mites, which are little black bugs that sometimes occur when the enclosure is not being kept up. Check your snake's mouth and nose area to ensure there's no mucus or runny nose type things coming from the mouth or nostril. Check the belly of your snake to ensure your heating pad is not turned up too high and that the snake is not burning itself. In other words, there are things you need to do to ensure the health of your snake on a daily, weekly, and monthly basis."*

Finding a reputable veterinarian or reptile specialist

You should ideally begin locating a trusted reptile vet before you ever get your first Ball Python. Depending on how you receive your Ball Python, it may require emergency care for any number of reasons that could have been unknown before you purchased the snake. You also will want to begin taking your Ball Python to the vet for regular check-ups to ascertain that it's healthy, growing, and that there are no early or chronic signs of illness present.

Having a reliable and trusted veterinarian on standby is vital to quickly and appropriately address any problems that may arise throughout your Ball Python's life. Local herpetology hobbyist organizations, Facebook groups, and forums may help you find a good vet in your area. Sleuthing through online reviews for nearby vet clinics may also give you a general idea of what to expect from a particular establishment.

Animal welfare organizations, zoos, breeders, and other animal and reptile professionals may be able to direct you to a trusted veterinarian. Once you find a trusted local reptile vet, it's important that you communicate as much information as you can about your Ball Python, its habits, and its condition. Listening to and following the vet's instructions is a big part of how to best keep your snake happy, healthy, and in the best possible condition.

The Association of Reptile and Amphibian Veterinarians' website (arav.org) has a helpful search tool under the "For Owners" tab that can help you find reptile vets in your area. It can also be a resource for general information, resources, and lectures on pet reptiles and amphibians.

Photo Courtesy of Pamela Green

CHAPTER 8

Conclusion and Further Resources

Ball Pythons, through their history and biology, are uniquely suited in the reptile world to be companions to humans, possibly even more so than many other species of snakes. Their tendency to have a docile temperament and relatively low-maintenance requirements make them fantastic pets for those who are willing to put in the work and are dedicated to their scaley friends' well-being. Each snake's unique personality helps make it an interesting learning experience. Combined with Ball Pythons' long life expectancy, they have many years of engaging companionship to offer dedicated owners.

Ball Pythons do not grow nearly as large as other constrictor snakes. For most people, this makes Ball Pythons much more accessible pets due to the higher costs, large housing space, and potential danger that might come along with larger species that might reach maximum sizes of 15 or 20 feet.

Compared to many other reptiles, Ball Pythons may be better suited to surviving comfortably in domestic life. The fact that they spend most of their time hidden and resting means they do not need as much daily exercise and stimulation as other animals with faster metabolisms. This inherently makes them well-suited for a laid-back life of domesticity with a knowledgeable and responsible owner. After all, Ball Python breeders sometimes manage to house dozens of snakes in fairly simple plastic tubs with relatively cheap and easy-to-accommodate conditions. You must know what you're doing when caring for a Ball Python, but once that is locked down and you've established best practices, care often does not present too many additional variables. Through attentiveness

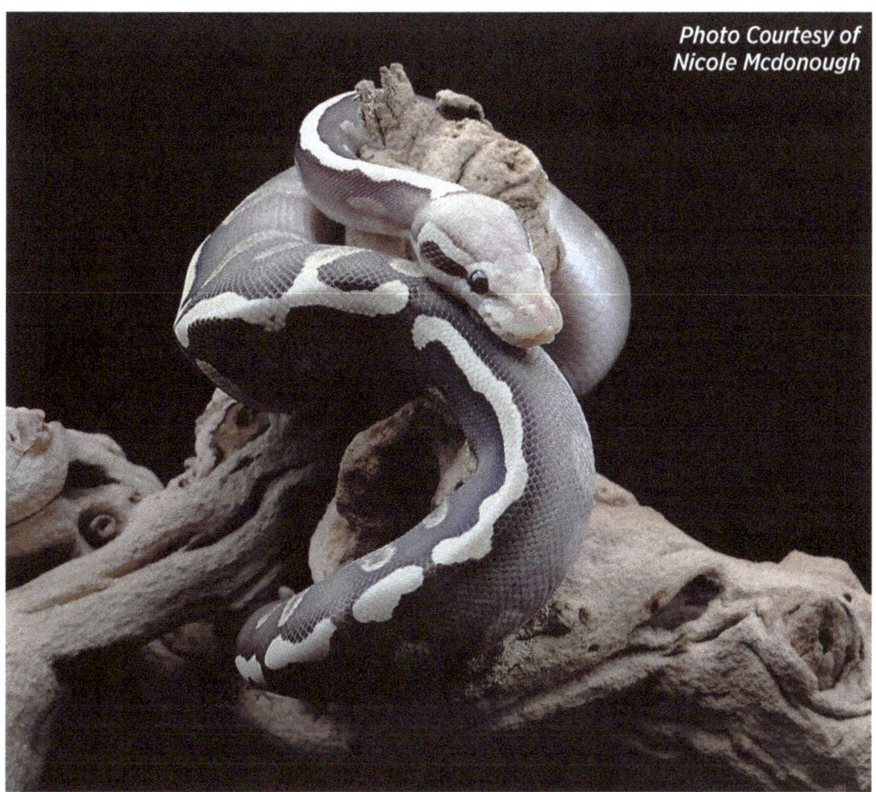

and thorough research, you can become a successful and responsible Ball Python owner in a relatively short amount of time.

The variability and striking appearance of Ball Python morphs also adds a unique "wow" factor. Few reptiles have similar variety in the morphs and physical differences which can present between different individuals in the species. For this reason, Ball Pythons are especially valued among reptile lovers.

"Ball Pythons make great pets for first-time snake owners," says Joanna Alzate-Sherksnas of CB Reptile in New Jersey. *"They are very friendly and calm if they are handled frequently. Some even seem to enjoy coming out of their tank to socialize with people. One of my own (his name is Hershey) will start cruising the sides of his tank if I am in the room, so I will go to open up the doors of the tank. I flatten my hand and put it near his neck, and almost every time he will put his head right into my palm and come on out. Ball*

Pythons are also very curious, so I enjoy being able to watch them explore when I take them out for some handling time. Sometimes they will find something interesting in the room and they'll spend a minute or two 'licking' it and gathering information about whatever object it may be. Their behavior will always be interesting for me to watch, even if I've seen it a million times."

Further Resources

Ball Pythons are capable of moving about one mile or 1.6 kilometers per hour over easy terrain. Because Ball Pythons don't chase their prey and rely on camouflage to protect themselves from predators, faster speeds aren't necessary. However, under duress, Ball Pythons can increase their speed slightly to escape a threat. Their slow pace makes these snakes excellent, calm pets for new snake owners.

Books and websites for further reading and research

A wealth of additional information about Ball Pythons can be found in books and websites through most online and physical retailers like Amazon or Barnes and Noble. Wikipedia is a go-to first resource for many just looking to learn the basics on many subjects. Ball Pythons are no different. The Wikipedia page for Ball Pythons has a lot of correct information for people curious about the history, biology, and basic information of Ball Python care, though Wikipedia may not be sufficient for any specific or in-depth questions. It's important to be aware that almost anyone can edit Wikipedia, and not all incorrect or suspect information may be caught by moderators. So be careful considering anything from the website as ironclad. As with anything, it's best to verify any information you find on Wikipedia with second and third sources, if possible.

A few examples of other websites that can be used to look up information on Ball Pythons are listed below:

www.worldofballpythons.com
reptilesmagazine.com
A-z-animals.com
www.xyzreptiles.com
Reptifiles.com
www.everythingreptiles.com

Many pet stores and Ball Python breeders also have websites where you can find specific information, recommendations, or access to live resources which may be able to better answer your questions.

Forums

There is a wealth of information and firsthand experience available online as long as you know where to look. Ball Python owners and breeders have created many spaces for both new and adept owners to converse and engage in discussion. With an unverified online resource, you have to take any advice with a grain of salt and understand that a post may be based more on opinion or individual experience rather than concrete fact or tried and tested methods. Generally, expert opinions and consensus should not be too difficult to weed out from bunk. If you have uncertainties with any claim, it can be helpful to check for additional sources to verify these questions. If the community or forum is currently active, you can often join in and ask questions yourself to fill in any gaps or clarify any desired information.

Some popular online communities and forums for support and advice are listed below:

www.reptilesforums.uk
www.Ball-pythons.net
Community.morphmarket.com
Forum.kingsnake.com
Ourreptilefourm.com
www.reddit.com/r/ballpython

A large number of YouTube channels also exist to disseminate infor-mation about Ball Pythons, give demonstrations, and answer commonly asked questions. For creators who frequently read comments or have methods of getting direct questions to answer in videos, their commu-nities can act much like most internet forums. Many Facebook groups, private and public, also seek to inform users and provide answers to commonly asked questions.

Local reptile clubs and organizations for socialization and education

Some people, especially those living in larger cities, may be lucky enough to find Ball Python or reptile clubs in their local area. For less populated areas, this may not be the case. You can try starting one of these organizations in your city or town yourself. The local reptile vet, Ball Python breeders, or pet stores may be good locations to talk to people and gauge community interest in these kinds of clubs. You may be able to put up posters in these areas with permission or even advertise in local newspapers to try and get other interested reptile owners to reach out. The utmost caution is required when trying to initiate or plan these meetups though. Be careful not to give out your location or too much sensitive information if you aren't comfortable with strangers having access to these things.

Reptile clubs can give you a support system to more readily and easily have your questions answered in case of emergencies. You can also see what level of success different owners have had in trying out different methods, setups, and techniques. Not to mention, other reptile owners may be able to point you toward good deals and additional resources. Having a community centered around a shared subject opens the doors for a whole new range of opportunities and friendships.

www.ingramcontent.com/pod-product-compliance
Lightning Source LLC
Chambersburg PA
CBHW040315030726
47513CB00040BB/291